Niagara

Niagara
Your Guide to the Falls and Beyond

RON BROWN

FIREFLY BOOKS

A Firefly Book

Published by Firefly Books Ltd. 2024
Copyright © 2024 Firefly Books Ltd.
Text copyright © 2024 Ron Brown
Photographs © as listed on this page and page 240

All rights reserved. No part of this publication may be reproduced, stored in a retrieval system, or transmitted in any form or by any means, electronic, mechanical, photocopying, recording or otherwise, without the prior written permission of the Publisher.

First Printing

Library of Congress Control Number: 2023946725

Library and Archives Canada Cataloguing in Publication
Title: Niagara : your guide to the Falls and beyond / Ron Brown.
Names: Brown, Ron, 1945- author.
Description: Includes index.
Identifiers: Canadiana 20230552552 | ISBN 9780228104643 (softcover)
Subjects: LCSH: Niagara (Ont. : Regional municipality)—Guidebooks. | LCSH: Niagara Falls (Ont.)—Guidebooks. | LCGFT: Guidebooks.
Classification: LCC FC3095.N5 B76 2024 | DDC 917.13/38045—dc23

Published in Canada by
Firefly Books Ltd.
50 Staples Avenue, Unit 1
Richmond Hill, Ontario
L4B 0A7

Published in the United States by
Firefly Books (U.S.) Inc.
P.O. Box 1338, Ellicott Station
Buffalo, New York
14205

Front Cover Photo Credits
Main image: Shutterstock/Sergii Figurnyi.
Inset images, from left to right: Ron Brown, Shutterstock/Harold Stiver, Shutterstock/Elena Berd, Shutterstock/Russ Heinl, Shutterstock/JHVEPhoto.

Printed in China | E

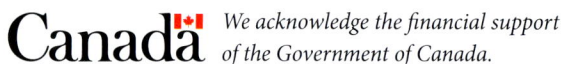

DEDICATION

This book is gratefully dedicated to the memory of my late parents, Ethel and Arnold Brown (RCN), for the unfailing support given to my siblings, Wayne and Barbara, and myself throughout their lives.
— Ron Brown

ACKNOWLEDGEMENTS

With a Little Help from My Friends

Authors of exploration guidebooks seldom succeed without considerable input from their "friends," those people who are more knowledgeable about the minutia of the many interesting places to visit and explore in the book. Here is a list of those organizations in and around Niagara Falls that helped me fill in the gaps in my knowledge:

Niagara Railway Museum, Fort Erie
Niagara Falls History Museum, Niagara Falls
Niagara Parks Commission, Niagara Falls
Niagara Parks Power Station, Niagara Falls
Mary Morton Tours
Maple Leaf Place, Niagara Falls
Canadian Railway Historical Association, (CRHA), Toronto and York Division
Henry of Pelham Estates Winery, Pelham
Magnotta Winery, Beamsville
Niagara on the Lake Tourism Office
Ravine Winery, Queenston
Niagara Falls Tourism
Old Stone Inn, Niagara Falls
Walker's Country Market, Niagara-on-the-Lake

CONTENTS

Introduction | 11

HISTORY AND HERITAGE
FALLING WATERS: The Evolution of the Falls at Niagara | **15**
TURTLE ISLAND: Niagara's Indigenous Legacy | **27**
FREEDOM TRAILS: Niagara's Black Heritage | **35**

WHERE TO GO AND WHAT TO SEE
SOMETHING FOR EVERYONE: Visiting Niagara Falls | **43**
SLEEPING OVER: Modern and Historic Hotels | **55**
DOWNTOWN NIAGARA: Historic Main Streets to Explore | **63**

NIAGARA'S FAMOUS ENTERTAINMENT DISTRICT
THAT'S ENTERTAINMENT: Tourism, from the Fractious Front to Midways and Casinos | **87**

WORLD-CLASS THEATRE AND VINEYARDS
THE PLAY'S THE THING: The Shaw Festival and the Arts | **101**
THE BEST GRAPES MAKE THE FINEST WINE: Niagara's Wine Country Trails | **109**

DAY TRIPS AND EXPLORATIONS – HISTORY
FLAMES ACROSS THE BORDER: The Legacy of the War of 1812 | **127**
GETTING AROUND: Niagara's Historic Highways | **141**
THE CASTLES OF THE CUESTA: Niagara's Historic Mansions | **153**
FORGOTTEN NIAGARA: Lost Villages and Ghost Towns | **163**

DAY TRIPS AND EXPLORATIONS – NIAGARA OUT OF DOORS
NATURE'S WONDERS: Niagara's Conservation Areas | **179**
CULTIVATED BEAUTY: Niagara's Formal Gardens | **187**
HAPPY TRAILS: Niagara's Walking and Hiking Trails | **195**

DAY TRIPS AND EXPLORATIONS – WATER AND RAIL
BRIDGING THE GAP: Niagara River Bridges | **209**
ENGINEERING MARVEL: The Welland Canal | **215**
RIDING THE RAILS: Niagara's Railway Legacy | **223**

Index | **234**
Photo Credits | **240**

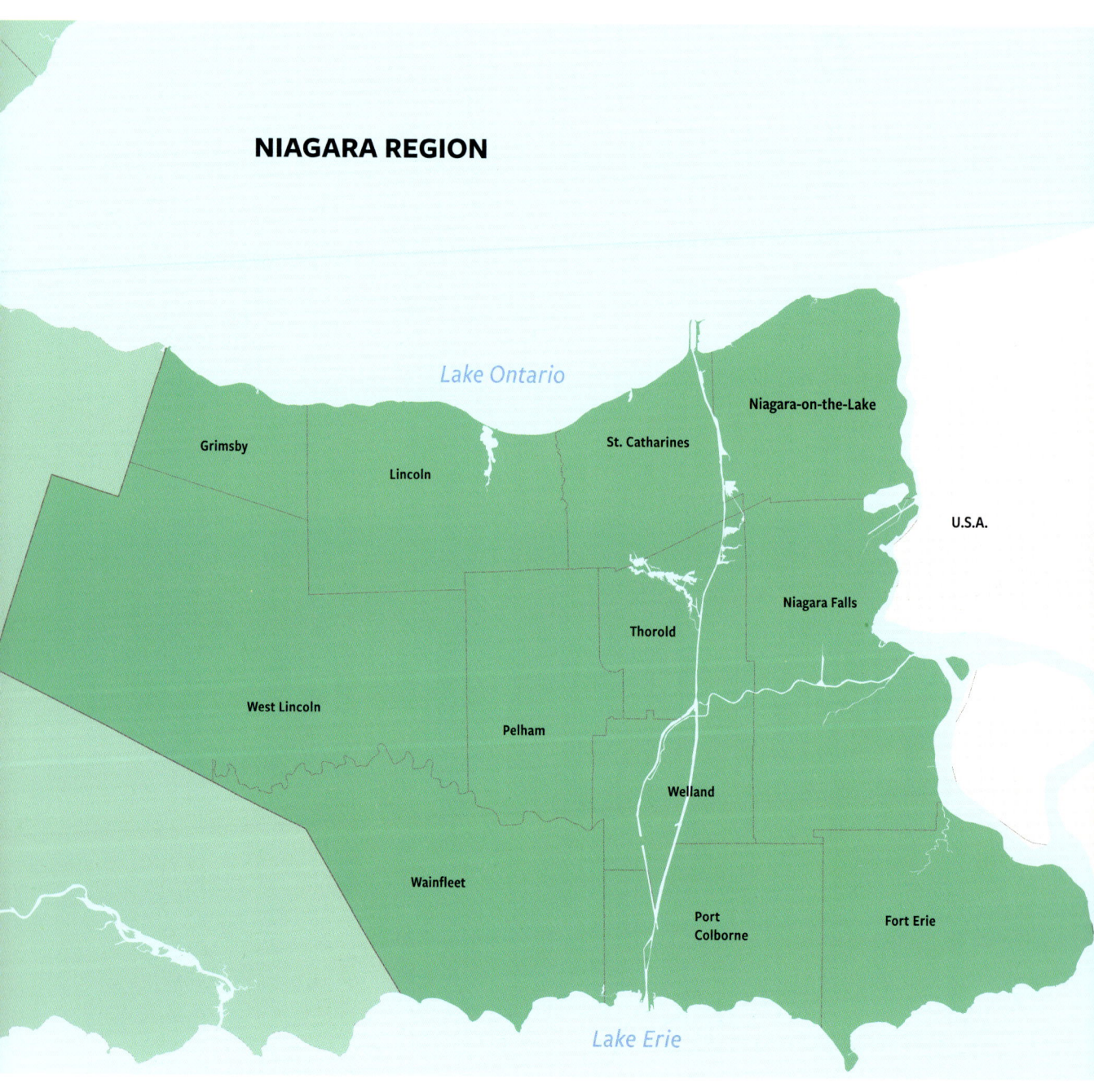

INTRODUCTION

An Explorer's Guide to Niagara Falls and the Lands Beyond

The first known European to gaze upon Niagara Falls was a Jesuit priest and explorer named Louis Hennepin in 1678. He took his somewhat exaggerated description of its size and power back to amazed Europeans. Later explorers made the sight a must-see, and most confirmed Hennepin's reports, although there were others who downplayed the falls, some even calling it "disappointing."

The last years of the 18th century saw an influx of people into the Niagara region for a different reason: fear of reprisals from the newly independent Americans who perpetrated assaults and theft upon those colonists who had remained loyal to Britain. These refugees were labelled by the British government as United Empire Loyalists and granted land in Ontario's border regions in recognition of their loyalty.

Conflict between the United States and Britain resumed in 1812 when the American military invaded the colonies of Upper and Lower Canada. After they were rebuffed and peace restored, tourism in Niagara began in earnest. As the decades advanced, railways arrived. The earliest was a horse-drawn trolley from Chippawa to Queenston as a portage railway in 1833, but with the arrival of the Great Western Railway in 1853, the tourist trade boomed.

With the arrival of the auto age, more and more visitors began to arrive and soon a visit became about more than just the falls itself and a new hotel boom took place. Amusements and theme parks and then casinos added to the allure. Today, this tiny peninsula has become one of Canada's leading tourist attractions.

But there is more to the Niagara region than the mighty cataract, more than the temptation of easy money in the casinos and more than the multitude of glitzy attractions. To go beyond the roar and the mist of Niagara Falls is to discover stunning viewpoints, historic battle sites from the last war fought on Canadian soil, a spider's web of hiking trails, curious rock formations, giant trees and other natural wonders and the engineering marvels of the Welland Canal, not to mention more than 90 wineries with their intoxicating treats.

This book is the story of the falls, as well as the story of Niagara beyond the falls.

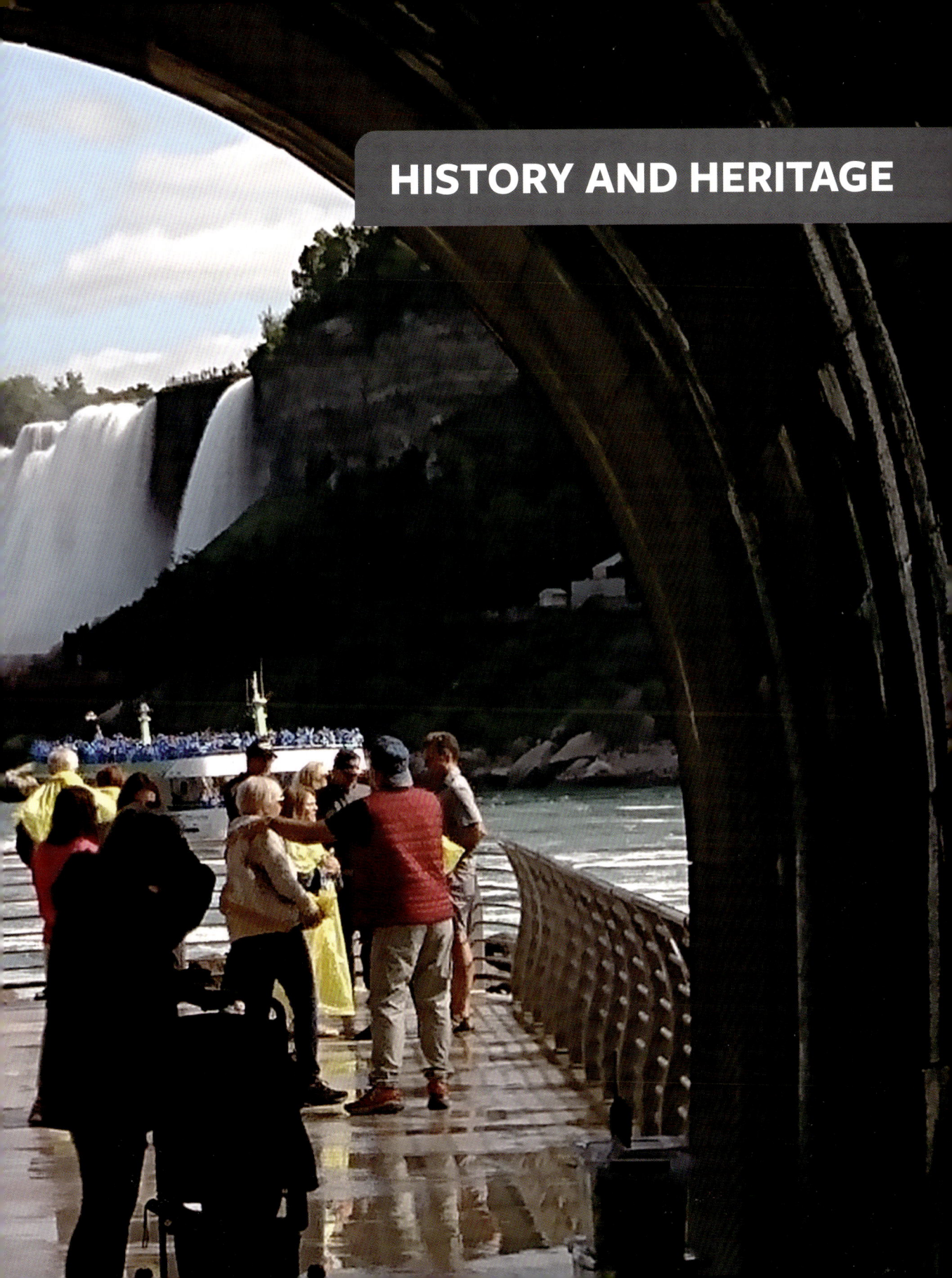

HISTORY AND HERITAGE

FALLING WATERS
The Evolution of the Falls at Niagara

The Bible tells us that the world was created in six days. The mighty falls at Niagara, however, took a little longer, about 12,000 years longer. But the Niagara Escarpment, over which the falls tumble, dates back much further than that, and, were it not for that escarpment, there would be no Niagara Falls at all.

About 450 million years ago, eastern North America was the site of a huge mountain range with peaks as lofty as Mount Everest. Over millions of years, erosion and glaciation wore them down to their roots. A few million years later, a tropical sea inundated the lands. Beneath those waters, layer upon layer of silt and sand was deposited onto the seabed. Over more millions of years those layers hardened into rock.

Four hundred million years ago, the sea gradually drained away and the rock layers began to erode. Erosion of these layers eventually resulted in the formation of the 900-kilometre-long cliff that we call the Niagara Escarpment, which stretches from Queenston to Tobermory. The distinctive cliff face of the falls is the result of a hard surface layer of dolomite sitting on top of softer layers of shale which eroded away below the hard top rock.

Previous spread: **Visitors can view the falls from the end of the Niagara Parks Power Station tailrace tunnel.**
Left: **The size and might of the falls dwarf the visiting tourists.**

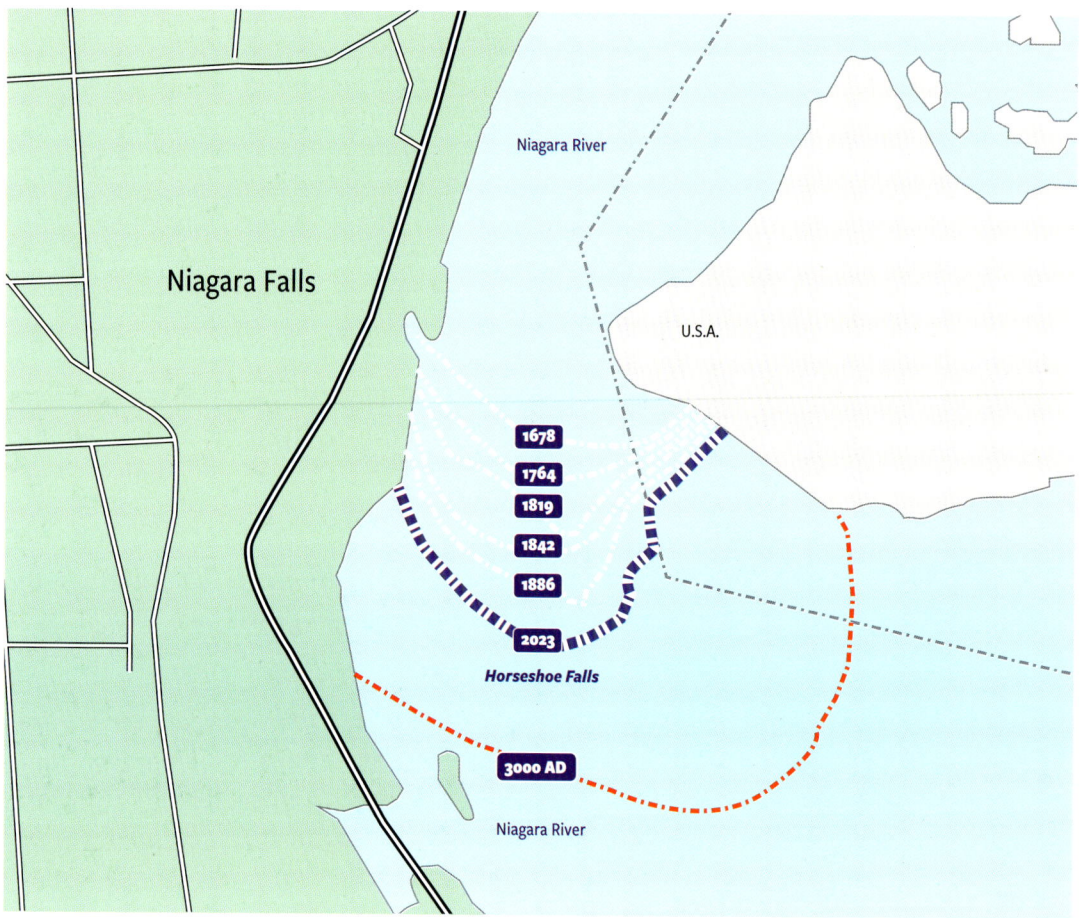

The force of the water pouring over the falls is constantly eroding the rock below the water. This illustration shows how the lip of the falls has receded over the years and a projection of where it will be in the year 3000 at the present rate of erosion.

The landforms which define the area today are a result of the Ice Ages. Snow accumulating over tens of thousands of years compacted into layers of ice which spread outward as the snow piled higher. The last Ice Age, which began around 100,000 years ago, blanketed most of the northern hemisphere with ice sheets which in places were two kilometres thick and extended well south of the area covered by today's Great Lakes.

Within the last 20,000 years, the earth began to warm again. The great glaciers thawed and gradually retreated northward. As they melted, they poured huge quantities of water onto the land. These torrents carved out valleys and collected behind the remaining barriers of ice, creating massive lakes, the precursors to today's Great Lakes. The water which became Lake Ontario was once 100 metres higher than the present lake level.

When the ice barrier blocking the

The Whirlpool Aero Car carries visitors over the swirling waters of the Niagara River.

water's exit into the St. Lawrence River melted away, the water level quickly fell to roughly the level of today's Lake Ontario.

Water began to flow across the land above the escarpment and plunged over the face of the cliff near today's Queenston. This marked the birth of Niagara Falls. The cascade which began at Queenston relentlessly ate into the rock layers over which it flowed and, after 10,000 years, the falls reached the point at which we see them today.

Hiking Through the Geology of the Great Gorge Today

Following the Niagara Parkway upstream from Niagara-on-the-Lake reveals the geological history of the Great Gorge and Niagara Falls.

A short distance south of Niagara-on-the-Lake, beside the Niagara Parkway, stands the McFarland House, a historic mansion built in 1800. Behind the house, a pathway leads to a small tributary creek which flows into the Niagara River. In the past, as the river eroded its way southward through the rocks of the escarpment, perhaps as many as 10 tributary streams spilled over the edge of the Niagara Gorge and into the Lower Niagara River.

As the Parkway continues to wind its

way southward, the cliffs of the escarpment loom closer. The marina at the village of Queenston offers a view of the ramparts through which the river makes its exit from the gorge. Following the glacier's retreat, it also signifies the location of the first falls.

Further up the steep escarpment, a lookout provides a wide view of the river and the plains below. Those plains, the bottom of old Lake Iroquois, are known as the Roy Terrace, so named in tribute to the geologist who researched the origins of the area. As Lake Iroquois retreated, it left behind a series of beach ridges, known today as terraces.

About 1.1 kilometres south of Queenston, there tumbles a mini-Niagara. In the ravine at Locust Grove Picnic Area, a stream falls six metres and then cascades down a talus of fallen boulders for a total drop of 74 metres. The site is within the Locust Grove Picnic Area on the east side of the Parkway, a short distance beyond the Queenston Heights traffic circle.

Past the entrance to Queenston Heights Park, a parking lot on the east side of the road, across from the famous Floral Clock, provides access to Smeaton's Ravine. The trail through the ravine reveals more secrets of the geological past. In this case, the ravine trail encounters a series of ledges where a post-glacial river tumbled into the emerging gorge.

Located near the top of the cliff, the first fall cascades 27 metres and the second another 12 metres, part of a total drop of 152 metres. Beyond these cascades, the water tumbles around and behind many fallen boulders as it makes its way into the river. The footing on the path is rugged and tricky and unmarked. At the river's edge, the ravine is cut off by roadways which lead to the adjacent Sir Adam Beck hydro plant.

Views Along the Gorge

Much more challenging, however, are the trails which mark the stunning and world-famous Niagara Glen. Four kilometres of trails spread out from the Nature Centre and trail guidebooks are available. The forests which line the route contain ancient tree species, many of them surviving northern outliers of the Carolinian forests to the south.

After crossing the undulating Wintergreen Flats, the trail suddenly comes to the edge of one of the park's cliffs where a high metal staircase leads to the more challenging paths below. Along the paths lie huge boulders which have broken free from the overhead cliffs by the freezing and expansion of water in the many fissures in the rock.

This is the process by which the falls has carved its way relentlessly to the point where it sits today. As the ice expands, the rocks break away and tumble into heaps below. The paths though Niagara Glen occasionally pass below those massive boulders, many of which are sufficiently steep that they have become popular with rock climbers.

Several of the lower trails are rated as difficult, suitable for only the most experienced hikers. These trails may involve

A difficult, rocky section along the Niagara Glen Trail.

crouching beneath boulders, following steep and slippery slopes and paths strewn with monstrous rocks. Many other trails have a moderate classification which, although tricky, are suitable for most hikers with some experience. The various routes eventually lead to the edge of the rushing and turbulent torrents, with the world's most daunting and terrifying rapids.

At the water's edge, a layer of soft red shale peeks out from beneath the lowest sedimentary layers; this is the visible remnant of that ancient mountain range upon which the escarpment formed. Among the cliffs, the remains of a coral reef remain from an ancient tropical sea.

A few metres beyond the Niagara Glen, a lane leads into the challenges of WildPlay Niagara, a playground with attitude. Across from the entrance to this playground, a short walk leads to Thompson Point and a stunning view of the whirlpool and the upper gorge.

A short distance south on the Parkway, beyond the WildPlay attraction, a small parking lot on the riverside allows access to a trail that makes its way down the St. David's Buried Gorge, the ancient pre-glacial course of an earlier river system. The glaciers filled the old gorge with the boulders and stones that they had picked up on their way. This trail leads through the most visible section of the St. David's Buried Gorge. The trails down the ravine lead to the riverbank, where the whirlpool swirls around. However, when water is low, there is insufficient flow for the whirlpool to form.

After passing through the urban portions of the city of Niagara Falls, the Parkway ultimately comes to the object of this geological tour, the great falls themselves. After 12,000 years, they are still receding and appear much different from those first viewed by Father Hennepin in 1688. In retreating back at a rate of several metres per year, they have now formed the elegant horseshoe shape that so entrances today's viewers. Yet even that is changing, as ongoing erosion has created a V-shaped crest in the middle of the horseshoe.

Table Rock

One of the most notable events of the falls' erosion was the documented collapse of Table Rock. Since tourists began arriving at the site in the early 1800s, Table Rock, an extensive ledge jutting out at the brink of the falls, offered a spectacular vantage point to admire the might of the falling water. In 1850, suddenly and without warning, the ledge cracked away and tumbled into the torrent, carrying with it a wagon and its unfortunate horse. The driver barely managed to escape. The remnant of the great rock rests partway down the cliff.

The American Falls is visually less appealing due to the talus heap at the base which now reaches more than halfway up the overall height of that falls. The cascade is narrower, with a straighter brink. If erosion continues unabated over the next millennia, both falls will eventually reach Lake Erie, turning the falls into a series of steep rapids.

Gates of the Gorge at Queenston, where the falls began to carve out the gorge 10,000 years ago.

Niagara's Electricity Story

Niagara isn't known only for fun and games, wineries, and the majestic cataract itself. Niagara also provides electricity for much of Ontario, and has done so since 1905.

The first to adopt the tremendous power of the river as an industrial power source was Daniel Decaire who, in 1759, diverted water from the river to turn a waterwheel for his sawmill.

By 1886, water was being diverted from the river above the falls to power industries along the edge of the gorge below the falls, primarily on the American side. However, separate canals and water turbines spewed unsightly waste water over the American brink and the scheme lacked any effective way to convert the power of the water to the electricity needed to drive those industries.

Many credit Thomas Edison for the invention of the electric light bulb. But it was a pair of British chemists named Warren de la Rue and Joseph Swan who discovered the means to convert electricity into light. On July 24, 1874 Canadians Henry Woodward and colleague Matthew Evans filed a patent for the first workable light bulb. Unable to market the device they sold the patent to inventor Thomas Alva Edison.

However, his light bulb used a form of electricity known as direct current, which was incapable of transmitting electricity great distances. It took a Croatian inventor named Nikola Tesla to devise a form of electricity, called alternating current, which was safer and more effective allowing electricity to be transmitted longer distances more economically.

In 1888, Tesla and George Westinghouse demonstrated the superiority of alternating current by lighting up 100,000 light bulbs at the 1893 Columbian Chicago World's Fair, a demonstration which Edison tried to block. After this display it became clear that alternating current was the wave of the future.

In 1892, William Birch Rankine created the Niagara Electric Power Company. In 1901, ground was broken to construct its power generating station at the lip of Niagara Falls. As water rushed in from the river, it plunged 60 metres to the turbines below and then exited through an 800 metre tailrace tunnel. Operations began in 1905 with five generators, later expanding to 11 in 1924.

The power station generated electricity until 2006, when it was decommissioned and acquired by the Niagara Parks Commission. Eventually the Parks Commission, recognizing the educational potential of the plant, opened it as a museum in 2020. In 2021, the tailrace tunnel was also opened to visitors. Today, it has become one the area's most popular attractions.

Visitors may purchase tickets and explore the history and workings of the plant, and then descend 60 metres by elevator to the tunnel. They then make their way through the 800-metre-long curving tunnel to the unparalleled view of both the Canadian and American falls from a platform at the base of the gorge.

Equally popular is the nighttime sound and light show, called Currents, where the entire 220-metre hall of the generating station is turned into a kaleidoscope of moving images that depict the evolution of Niagara

The beautiful Toronto Power Generating Station is a National Historic Site of Canada and the site of a proposed boutique hotel.

from the ice age to the electric age. The light show takes place in the hall itself.

But this is not the sole vestige of Niagara's electrical heritage. A few hundred metres south along the parkway stands the now vacant Toronto Power Generating Station. The plant opened in 1906 and was the only power plant in Niagara Falls to be owned by the Canadian government. Designed by noted architect E.J. Lennox, architect of Toronto's Old City Hall, it was decommissioned in 1974. It still contains the wheel pit, which houses the turbines, and its tailrace tunnel. Its classical pillars and more elaborate façade make it more visually striking than the Niagara Parks station. Although it was designated a National Historic Site in 1983, it remains mothballed until possible plans to repurpose it for its historic value are approved.

The Sir Adam Beck Power Plant

So, with these two power plants no longer in service, where does today's electric power come from? The answer to that lies downstream at the Sir Adam Beck Power Plants 1 and 2.

When its turbine whirled into action in 1922, the 18-storey Beck 1 was the world's largest power plant. Known by its original name, the Queenston-Chippawa Hydroelectric Plant, it became the world's largest publicly owned power plant. In 1950, it was renamed the Sir Adam Beck 1 Generating Station and could produce 12,300 gigawatts of energy. Because of its distance from the falls, a large area of land was turned into ponds and reservoirs from which the water

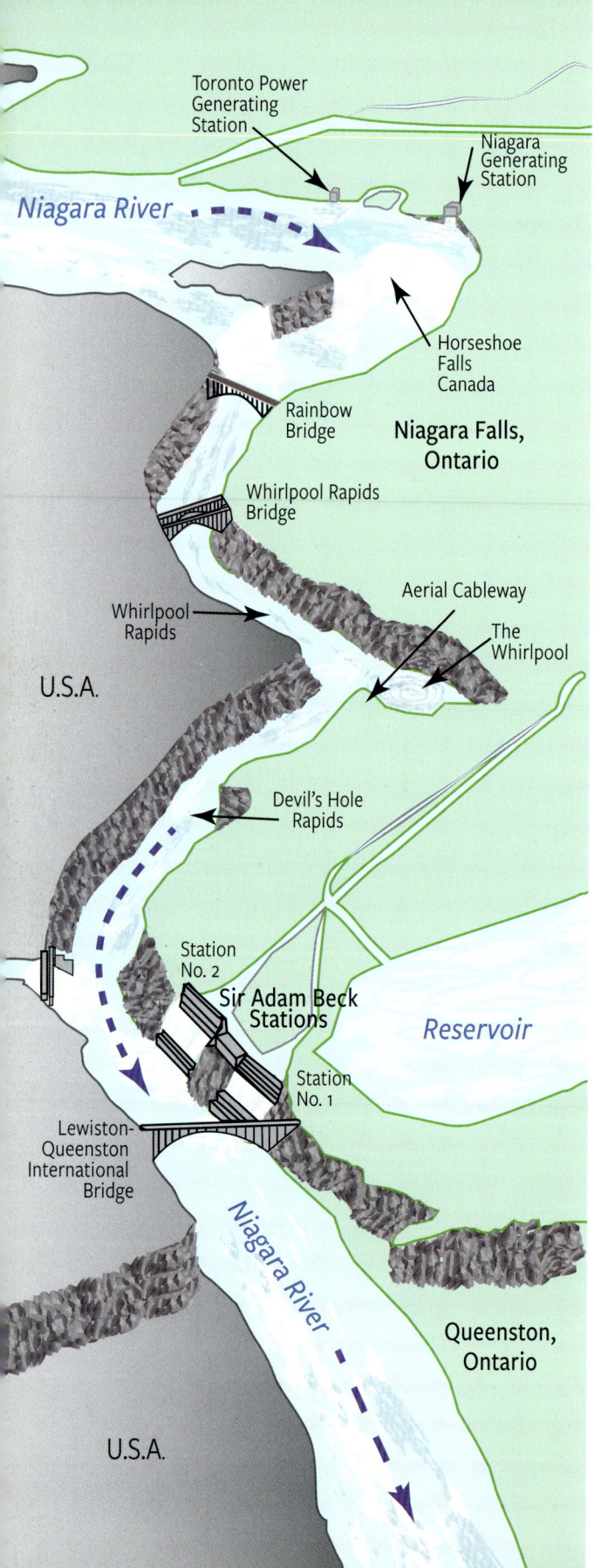

plunges down the penstocks to drive the turbines below. It was designated a National Historic Site of Canada in 1990 and is an important part of Ontario Power Generation's power grid.

In 1954, Beck 2 whirred into service, using a massive reservoir that received water from the Welland River at Chippawa. The water flows through a long canal, which feeds a massive reservoir above the plant. Ontario Hydro now has two water tunnels that traverse the entire city of Niagara Falls from the Village of Chippawa in the south to the Sir Adam Beck Hydroelectric Generating Stations.

While the Ontario Power Generation property is off-limits to the public, the older hydro canal is visible from a number of bridges throughout the city. At night, when hydro control dam gates are lifted for diversion of the Niagara River water into the hydro tunnels, the flow over the Horseshoe Falls drops to a minimum 15,240 cubic metres of water per second. The Ontario Hydro water intake gates for water diversion are located 2.6 kilometres upstream from the Horseshoe Falls.

Although tours of the Beck facility have been discontinued, the Niagara Parkway, which runs in front of the Beck plants, gives awestruck viewers a good idea of how massive these structures really are. A pullover area beside the Parkway just south of the plant offers the only roadside viewpoint available of the massive structure. Across the gorge, the multiple layers of bedrock reveal the timelines for the evolution of the escarpment itself. The view also takes in the Robert Moses Niagara Power Plant on the American side of the river.

Left: **This illustration shows the location of the major features along this stretch of the Niagara River.**

Above: **The newly restored turbines at the Niagara Parks Power Station, now open to visitors.**

TURTLE ISLAND
Niagara's Indigenous Legacy

Indigenous mythology tells the story of how the earth was created on the back of a giant turtle. To this day, Indigenous legends refer to our land as Turtle Island.

12,000 years ago, the landscape in what is now Ontario was a tundra-like barrens populated with northern animal species such as elk and caribou. On the heels of the retreating ice sheets, people, known as Mound Builders, also migrated north from what is today's Ohio. The serpent mounds of the Rice Lake area and mounds in northwestern Ontario are evidence of their presence.

Then, around 700 CE (Current Era), Iroquoian people, with their practice of corn cultivation, began migrating into the Niagara area, displacing the Algonquian people who had moved northward. Archaeological research on Grand Island in the Niagara River has unearthed evidence, including ceramics and spear points, of earlier occupations of the area, which they have dated from between 900 to 500 BCE (Before Current Era).

In the heart of Queenston Heights Park, the Landscape of Nations monument pays tribute to the Indigenous legacy of the region and to the part the First Nations' warriors played in the War of 1812.

The First Nations Peace Monument at the DeCew House Heritage Park, Thorold.

When the European exploration of the area was beginning around 1600, Niagara was home to the Neutral Confederacy, a coalition of eight or 10 tribal groups numbering about 40,000 people living in upwards of 30 villages over a wide area.

These groups included the Chonnonton and Onguiaahra peoples, the latter of which meant "near the big waters" and after whom the Europeans gave the region the name "Niagara." They referred to themselves as the Haudenosaunee, or people of the longhouse, and engaged in the cultivation of beans, corn, and squash, known as the "three sisters" of agriculture at the time.

Their mythology recounts that the falls originated when a giant evil serpent swimming upstream was killed by the benevolent God of Thunder. The horn and tail of the serpent were caught in the rocks, creating the horseshoe shape of the falls.

Another legend about the Maid of the Mist originated with the Seneca people; in the legend a Seneca woman saves her people by sacrificing herself. She became known as the Maid of the Mist, a name later given to a long-standing boat excursion to the base of the falls. The excursion on the Canadian side of the falls is now called the Hornblower.

By 1655, raids into Ontario by the Iroquois of New York had led to the dispersal of not only the Neutral Nation, but also the Wyandot people further north. Beginning in the 1700s, when the area was under British rule, the area's Indigenous populations were coerced into surrendering their territories and accepting a life on reserves which deprived them of their traditional lands and livelihood.

Because of the transitory nature of the First Nations occupation of the land, little physical evidence of their presence survives. Nevertheless, in recent years, greater recognition of Indigenous peoples' values and legacies has resulted in recognition of Indigenous sites in a number of locations throughout the Niagara region.

The Ossuary

One of the earliest discoveries of the legacy of the region's original inhabitants occurred in 1828 following a violent windstorm. A large tree in the area of St. David's blew down, revealing among its tangle of roots one of Ontario's largest ossuaries, an Indigenous burial ground. Regrettably, in those days, there was little appreciation of the sacred nature or archaeological value

Kanien'keha:ka is the traditional name of the Mohawk people.

of these places and everything, including the bones and artifacts, was carted away as souvenirs, and the site remained largely ignored. Subsequent excavations, including those for a subdivision, removed all further traces.

The large deposit of bones at this location suggests that since there is no record of an Indigenous community here, and the fact that burials only took place every 7 or 8 years, they were brought here from other places solely for burial purposes.

While the Ossuary may have been obliterated, it was not entirely forgotten. In 1934, the Lundy's Lane Historical Society erected a four-metre-high stone cairn topped with a carved limestone arrowhead, pointing in the direction of the Ossuary site. Two plaques on it describe the story of the Ossuary, as well as the locations of the home of Upper Canada's one-time Lieutenant Governor Sir Peregrine Maitland. The cairn is tucked into a small grassy area at the southwest corner of Pinestone Road and St. Paul Avenue in the north end of Niagara Falls. It is now surrounded by a housing development.

The Indian Village

As tourism grew in the 1950s and 1960s, Ontario's First Nations peoples became potential tourist attractions. In 1960, the Niagara Falls Indian Village opened and billed itself as "an authentic Iroquois village" although it was not on any actual First Nations village site. The village consisted of replica palisades, wigwams, a sweat lodge and longhouse as well as a

log cabin relocated from the Six Nations territory on the Grand River. Guides were hired from the Six Nations of the Grand River First Nation to recount Indigenous traditions and perform various traditional dances. But in 1961 the Indian Village gained a new neighbour, Marineland and Game Farm. Attendance declined, lured by newer attractions, and the village closed in 1968, with the land becoming part of the Marineland property.

Norton's Cabin

Another artifact from Indigenous times is the cabin built by Chief John Norton in 1817. Half Cherokee and half Scot, Norton was mentored by Joseph Brant of the Grand River Mohawks, and was instrumental in participating in numerous attacks on American forces during the 1812 war. As such, he is considered one the war's First Nations heroes.

Originally built on the Six Nations territory on the Grand River, the cabin was moved to its current location beside the historic Brown Homestead in 1997 to preserve its legacy.

In 2011, the Historic Sites and Monuments Board of Canada designated Norton a "Person of National Historic Significance;" in other words, a hero. The Homestead and cabin are on Regional Road 81, opposite the entrance to the Short Hills Provincial Park.

Today, a cairn commemorates the location of an ancient ossuray near St. David's.

Landscape of Nations

One of the more visited of Niagara's Indigenous monuments is the Landscape of Nations Memorial near the Brock Monument in Queenston Heights Park. It is dedicated to Britain's First Nations allies who helped the British and Canadians to repel American attacks at Queenston Heights. The display includes life-size bronze statues of John Brant (son of Joseph Brant) and John Norton, both led their warriors in terrifying attacks on the enemy.

The memorial is full of symbolism; the Memory Circle includes walls of 400-million-year-old limestone extracted from the nearby Queenston Quarry that extend outward in a sunburst pattern. Stone walkways are designed to resemble the two-row wampum belt marking the peace treaty between the Haudenosaunee and the Europeans. The memorial also commemorates the Peace and Reconciliation ceremony of August 31-September 1, 1815, which restored peace among the many nations involved in the War of 1812. Located in the centre of the memorial is a turtle that represents the Earth in the Indigenous story of creation. Entrance to the circle is through a series of arches meant to represent a longhouse, since the Haudenosaunee are known as the "people of the longhouse."

Unveiled in Queenston in 1980, the Six Nations Warriors Plaque honours the Haudenosaunee Confederacy for its

A large bronze statue in the Landscape of Nations Monument pays tribute to Chief John Norton who successfully led the Mohawk warriors against the invading American forces.

involvement at the Battle of Queenston Heights on October 13, 1812. The plaque tells the story of John Brant and John Norton, two key Indigenous leaders during the battle. The plaque sits on a granite boulder on Queenston Street, just west of Brock's Monument in Queenston.

First Nations Peace Monument

Another important First Nations monument sits in DeCew House Heritage Park, south of St. Catharines. The First Nations Peace Monument is a memorial designed by world-renowned architect and human rights activist Douglas Cardinal. It is situated near the site where Laura Secord encountered First Nations warriors who assisted her in conveying a warning of an impending American invasion to the colonial British forces. Displaying Cardinal's distinctive curvilinear design, the monument was unveiled in 2017.

Norton's Grove

Norton's Grove in Fort Erie marks the location of the site where Indigenous allies supported British forces during the War of 1812. The British troops and Indigenous warriors were led by Major John Norton, an adopted Haudenosaunee leader, during Drummond's night assault on August 15, 1814. Norton's Grove is located on the north side of Dominion Road, across the street from Old Fort Erie.

At the Old Fort Erie historical site, a display of Haudenosaunee craftsmanship includes an original knife sheath worn by Jacob Servos during the American Revolution.

Mewinzha Archaeology Gallery

A somewhat unlikely location for a display of First Nations artifacts is the display in the Mewinzha (meaning "a long time ago") Archaeology Gallery in the Peace Bridge Administration Building. The gallery honours the First Nations peoples who lived at the site. Artifacts found here date back 11,000 years and were recovered from excavations and archeological digs in the Fort Erie area. Many of the artifacts were found by Parks Canada archaeologists on nearby Navy Island. Accompanying them is a display of contemporary artworks that recount various Indigenous stories.

The British Indian Department Indian Council House

This structure, built in 1796 near Fort George, is where the Haudenosaunee Confederacy (Six Nations) and other Indigenous allies gathered for councils, treaty negotiations and to receive annuities from the British Crown. The building was destroyed during the War of 1812, but was rebuilt in 1815. Although the structure no longer exists, a series of commemorative markers at the site, referred to as The Commons, commemorates the building and its role in the early relations between the region's First Nations and the colonizing governments. After 1828, the building became a military post on the grounds of Butler's Barracks. The location in Niagara-on-the-Lake is owned and operated by Parks Canada.

Indigenous people knew much about the land on which they dwelled. To acknowledge this stewardship in 2017, the Niagara

Parks Commission created a series of 12 Indigenous-inspired pollinator gardens along the Niagara Parkway. These range from formal manicured gardens to natural habitats. The gardens feature the works of Haudenosaunee artists that include animal legends and Ontario's native species. The collection was inspired by the Haudenosaunee Confederacy (Iroquois), the Wabanaki Confederacy (Algonquin) and Anishinaabe.

Niagara College Indigenous Garden

In June of 2018, the Welland and Niagara-on-the-Lake campuses of Niagara College became the sites of Indigenous gardens. The gardens include traditional plants once common in Indigenous villages in southern Ontario including the traditional three sisters planting of corn, beans, and squash. The gardens also include plants such as cedar, white sage, sweetgrass and tobacco, which were used in ceremonies. The gardens were designed by horticulturalist Teri Sherwood, a member of the Oneida Nation of the Thames.

St. Catharines Totem Pole

Although totem pole carving was never part of Ontario's Indigenous tradition, a genuine totem pole was placed in St. Catharines' Centennial Gardens in 1966 as part of the city's celebration of Canada's centennial. The 10.7-metre-tall totem pole was designed and carved by Kwakwaka'wakw

Visitors to the Niagara College Indigenous Garden learn about First Nations conservation techniques.

artist Doug Cranmer of the 'Namgis First Nation in British Columbia. Over the years, the totem pole has deteriorated, and city council decided to restore it and reinstall it in Richard Pierpoint Park along the Merritt Trail near downtown St. Catharines.

In 2021, Niagara Falls gained a new Indigenous mural by First Nations muralist Leona Skye-Grandmond. Located on the facade of the Third Space Café on Queen Street, the image conveys traditional First Nations ways of teaching.

FREEDOM TRAILS
Niagara's Black Heritage

Niagara's Black history began not with the Underground Railroad, but rather with the American War of Independence. When the 13 American colonies rebelled against British rule, those loyal to the Crown fled northward into the Canadian colonies to escape persecution from their former neighbours. Many brought with them their household slaves. Other African Americans found themselves on Canadian soil as a result of helping the British military during the Revolutionary War and, later, the War of 1812. These Black veterans were freed and given land upon which to settle, many of whom settled in and around today's Niagara-on-the-Lake.

The colony's first governor, John Graves Simcoe, had earlier attempted to end slavery in the colony but was opposed by the slave holders and had to content himself with banning only the slave trade through the 1793 Act to Limit Slavery. Slavery was eventually abolished throughout the entire British Empire in 1838.

For over 50 years, beginning as early as 1796, more than 40,000 slaves came to make their home in Canada. The famous Underground Railroad movement began as the result of two events, the

The Voices of Freedom Park in Niagara-on-the-Lake commemorates the legacy of the Underground Railroad.

One of the more popular Underground Railroad crossing points between the United States and Canada was at Fort Erie. It was close to the American shore, and the river was not as perilous as further north. Here, ferry operators from Buffalo, New York, often aided fugitive slaves and used a secret system of codes and symbols to distinguish bona fide passengers from potential slave kidnappers. A plaque situated on a large rock next to the Niagara Parkway in Fort Erie commemorates this crossing point.

Freedom Park

Close by, near the Niagara Parks Marina in Fort Erie, is Freedom Park and the Bertie Street Ferry Landing. The landing was the longest operating ferry dock used by freedom seekers and the site where thousands of fugitive slaves first set foot in Canada.

The freed slaves established themselves in their new settlements. A plaque on the south side of the marina describes one such now-vanished settlement, known as Little Africa. In the 1840s, most of the residents were employed in cutting wood for the wood burning ferries and then for the steam locomotives on the railway. The settlement of Little Africa flourished until 1875, reached a peak population of 200 and included its own church and stores. After coal began to replace wood as a source of fuel most of the community began to disperse. A cemetery known as the "Coloured Cemetery" was part of the community and exists to this day. It is located at the corner of Curtis Lane and Ridgemount Road, a short distance west of Fort Erie. The laneway which leads to it, a

The British Methodist Episcopal Church, in Niagara Falls, Ontario, was instrumental in bringing fleeing American slaves to freedom in Canada.

abolition of slavery throughout the British Empire in 1838 and the enactment of the Fugitive Slave Act in the United States in 1850 that allowed for the capture and return of escaped slaves.

few metres north of the historic St. John's Anglican Church, is a narrow dirt road and difficult to identify from Ridgemount Road.

African Americans had been arriving in the Niagara region since 1788. Most were followers of the African Methodist Episcopal Church and, in 1820, erected a small chapel in St. Catharines which became a major destination for African American arrivals.

Construction of the new Welland Canal forced the group to relocate their chapel, and in 1837 a new church opened. But by 1850 growing numbers of former slaves following the Underground Railroad meant a still larger church was needed. In 1855, the present chapel was opened.

It was designated a National Historic Site of Canada in 1999. In 2005, Harriet Tubman was designated a Person of National Historic Significance. In 2013, the PBS TV network featured the modest chapel in an award-winning documentary, *The African Americans: Many Rivers to Cross*.

In 1850, the American government, capitulating to angry slave owners, enacted the Fugitive Slave Act, which allowed for the arrest of escaped slaves, even in Canada. Harriet Tubman, who had escaped her brutal servitude a year earlier, began to heroically lead slaves to the American free states and then across the Niagara River to safe houses in Fort Erie. She established her base of operations in St. Catharines where she lived from 1850 until 1862. In 1862 Tubman moved to Auburn, New York where she died in 1913.

Fort Erie's "Coloured Cemetery" lies along a dirt road west of the town.

Posters like this warned former slaves who had escaped to Canada that they still faced danger.

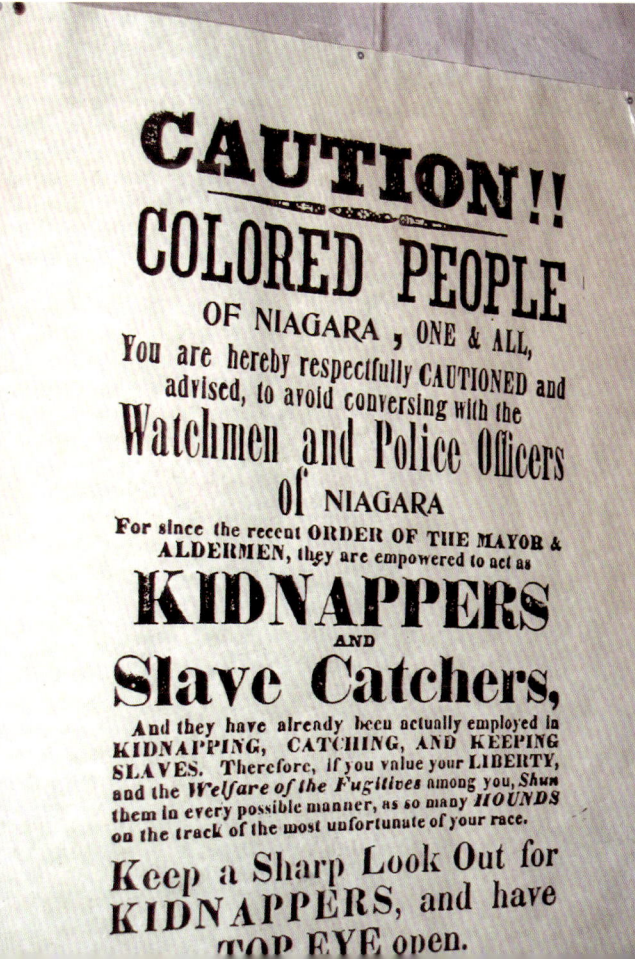

A tribute to Tubman stands by the chapel which is situated at 92 Geneva Street in St. Catharines. There is a public school named in her honour on Henry Street. Tributes to this brave woman are also situated at the entrance to the White Water Trail in Niagara Glen just north of Niagara Falls.

One of the many safe havens for travellers on the Underground Railroad in Niagara Falls was the Nathaniel Dett Chapel at 5674 Peer Street. The chapel was constructed in 1836 on Murray Street in the Fallsview area and later rolled on logs to a site in the present Drummondville area. It was recognized as a National Historic Site of Canada in 2000.

Niagara-on-the-Lake contains many sites of significant Black history. One such site is the Steward Home at Butler and John Streets. William Steward was one of 17 people who signed a petition asking Lieutenant Governor Sir Francis Bond Head to refuse to extradite a Kentucky fugitive slave named Solomon Moseby who was earlier rescued from the Niagara jail by more than 200 community members.

Another significant site, located on Mississauga Street near the corner of John Street West, is the Niagara Baptist Church Burial Ground, which dates from 1830. Ground-penetrating radar has determined that 28 bodies lie in the cemetery, while 19 headstones also lie under the soil.

Niagara Movement

However, the abolition of slavery in the United States in 1863 did not end the fight for freedom for Black Americans. In July of 1905, a group of 28 Black men, known at that time as the Niagara Movement, crossed the Niagara River from Buffalo, New York and landed at Fort Erie. Theirs was an organization dedicated to obtaining equal rights for African Americans. After rejecting Buffalo as a meeting location, the members chose the Erie Beach Hotel located in the Erie Beach Amusement Park, a short distance west of Fort Erie.

Many early historians have claimed that their choice of Fort Erie was due to discrimination by hotel owners in Buffalo. Later researchers have determined that the site was chosen due to its quieter location far from the curious citizenry. The Niagara Movement eventually evolved into the National Association for the Advancement of Coloured People (NAACP), which was founded a few years later in New York State. The hotel was part of the Erie Beach Amusement Park. Ruins of the park structures lie amid the woodlands of Waverly Beach Park. Among the historic plaques at the park's entrance is one which outlines the evolution of the Niagara Movement and its history at the park.

Voices of Freedom Park

Niagara's Voices of Freedom Park opened in 2018. An experiential art display leads visitors along pathways through the park to learn about the Black experience. The opening date of the site commemorates the 225th anniversary of the Act to Limit Slavery in Upper Canada. The park is located at the corner of Regent and Johnson Streets and was designed by Tom Ridout, OALA.

St. Mark's Church on Byron Street contains records of the town's Black

A small dwelling located in what was once the "coloured" section of Niagara-on-the-Lake.

population. The cemetery here contains the remains of early Black townspeople, and members of the Coloured Corps. The church was completed in 1810, but needed reconstruction following severe damage by American troops during the War of 1812. Restoration was finished in 1828.

The building called the "Slave Cottage" at 243 Gate Street was the residence of a man who never was a slave. Built in 1837 by Daniel Waters, a livery stable owner, it sits in what was known as the "Coloured Village," a community of early Black freedom seekers.

The Winnifred House at 309 Victoria Street was owned by Winnifred Wesley, granddaughter of freedom seeker George Wesley. She and her family members owned several properties throughout the town.

At 507 Butler Street a simple cottage was the residence of William and Susannah Seward. It too is situated in the part of town once known as the "Coloured Village."

The Niagara Commission's publication *Black History Along the Niagara River* lists a number of other Black heritage sites along its roads and trails.

WHERE TO GO AND WHAT TO SEE

SOMETHING FOR EVERYONE
Visiting Niagara Falls

Often listed as one of the natural wonders of the world, Niagara Falls is among the most popular destinations for visitors from Canada, the United States, and around the world. More than 12,000,000 visitors a year come to the Canadian side of the falls and another 8,000,000 a year visit the American side. This enormous number of visitors watch as 6 million cubic feet of water flows over the Canadian falls every minute of peak flow — an amount equal to about one million bathtubs filled to the brim.

One category of visitors has become an iconic symbol of the falls' popularity — honeymooning couples. More than 50,000 newlyweds visit the falls each year, keeping up a tradition that began all the way back in 1804, when Napoleon's brother brought his bride to see the falls on their tour of North America.

Niagara's Busy River Road
No matter where you stay, there are plenty of places to view the falls and other attractions located along River Road. River Road is a section of the Niagara Parkway that runs through the city of

Left: **Visitors stand in awe at the very edge of Niagara Falls.**

Previous page: **The light show on the falls at night.**

The iconic Carillon Tower is part of the Customs Plaza on Niagara's River Road.

Niagara Falls. The extensive attractions found along the Parkway are covered in detail later in this book.

Table Rock Welcome Centre

Pretty much every visitor to the falls for many generations has begun their visit at the Table Rock Welcome Centre. Table Rock itself was a projecting slab of stone that provided a natural viewing platform. However, in 1850, it gave way beneath a driver and his wagon, hurling the horse and wagon onto the rocks below, while the terrified driver barely escaped the plunge.

Use of this commanding site dates to 1827. Thomas Barnett, taking advantage of the spectacular location, constructed the Table Rock Museum closer to the falls' brink than today's structure. He added a staircase which led down the side of the cliff to the foot of the cascade. Other businesses quickly followed and soon there was a row of sleazy taverns and cheap hotels lining the brink and was known as The Front.

This all changed with the passing of the Niagara Falls Park Act in 1885. Under the new law, all privately owned properties on the land were purchased by the Ontario government, with most structures being demolished. Due to its prime location and relatively good condition, the Table Rock House was retained.

When the park officially opened on May 24, 1888, it became the park's flagship visitor building. In 1925, construction began on a new Table Rock House closer to the brink of the falls.

After exploring the Table Rock Welcome Centre, visitors can enjoy the many attractions found along River Road within the city of Niagara Falls. Many visitors start their tour of the city at Maple Leaf Place at the northern end of River Road, about five kilometres from Table Rock House, and continue along River Road until they get to Old Scow Lookout Point at the southern end of the road beyond the falls.

The Niagara River Parkway then resumes its tranquil route from the oasis that is Dufferin Islands up the wide river to historic Fort Erie.

Maple Leaf Place and the Ten Thousand Buddhas

What is more Canadian than moose and maple syrup? The Maple Leaf Place attraction offers not only a wide variety of maple syrup, but also an opportunity to learn the history and techniques for making maple syrup.

A few paces beyond the moose and the maple syrup, is the entrance to the Sarira Stupa Temple, also known as the Ten Thousand Buddhas. This striking 7-storey structure with its flared temple rooflines and gilded windows, contains 10,000 Buddha statues around the grounds and in the temple; one of them is five storeys high.

White Water Walk

Two kilometres north of Table Rock Centre on the river side, the entrance to the White Water Walk invites visitors to descend to the river level in elevators to experience the power and force of the world's fiercest rapids.

The road then reaches a portion of the city which has seen better days as it goes beneath the Whirlpool Bridge. The structure was built in 1897 to accommodate rail traffic along the top deck while vehicles and pedestrians use the lower deck.

To the west of the bridge, Bridge Street is a reminder of the days when the railroad was very important to Niagara. The former hotels and restaurants, which catered to visitors arriving across the early bridge or by rail, are now closed and shuttered.

By contrast, a few blocks away the historic Queen Street core area still contains several historic stores and buildings. The WEGO hop-on-hop-off bus shuttle departs right across Bridge Street from the historic and still functioning VIA Rail/GO train station. The shuttle goes to many of the more popular tourist stops in and around the city.

Then the River Road encounters yet another historic railway bridge just a few

The Sarira Stupa Temple contains a 12-metre-tall statue of the Buddha.

Among the first of many tightrope walkers to brave the dizzying heights above the Niagara River was Charles Blondin (left) in 1859; the latest was Nik Wallenda in 2012. Unlike previous rope walkers, Wallenda was tethered to a safety harness.

metres away; it is the now-abandoned Michigan Central Railroad Bridge, built in the same steel arch style as the Whirlpool Bridge. This bridge opened in 1925, replacing the Niagara Cantilever Bridge that stood there from 1883 to 1925.

The River Road then leads past Niagara's historic mansion row, where grand homes from the late 19th and early 20th centuries look from their hilltop location over the gorge. The rise of land on which these homes sit is a pre-historic riverbank dating from the time thousands of years ago when the waters of Lake Erie were much higher than those of today and flowed northward through a wider river, creating a bank above today's gorge.

Along this section of River Road, aside from a few motels, are historic homes, several of which have been repurposed themselves as inns or B&Bs. Early mansions like the Niagara Inn, the Niagara Gorgeview, and Niagara Luxury Suites offer a more tranquil accommodation experience than might be found in the city's core.

Then abruptly, at Phillips Street, the landscape changes into a modern scene, with a Travelodge Inn and the Bird Kingdom attraction dominating the street.

Rainbow International Bridge

River Road then passes under the Rainbow International Bridge. The Customs plaza here is worth a look. Opened in 1941, the architecture consists of a curved plaza with the Rainbow Tower looming above. The 50-metre tower opened in 1947 and features

The beauty of Queen Victoria Park provides a fitting background to the falls.

The Niagara Falls Incline Railway was constructed in 2013 as a shortcut linking the Fallsview district above the bluff with Table Rock Welcome Centre.

a 55-bell carillon which resonates across the falls three times daily. The location was featured in the iconic Marilyn Monroe movie *Niagara* in 1953.

One street back from River Road, Falls Avenue leads past the historic General Brock Hotel and Casino Niagara, as well as a new waterpark. At Clifton Hill, the road comes to the elegant Oakes Garden Theatre, an open-air amphitheatre with curved bench seating, concrete archways and a spectacular seasonal floral display. Opened in 1937, it is often considered the gateway to Queen Victoria Park.

This, then, is the foot of Clifton Hill. In the early days it went by the name of Ferry Street when it terminated at the ferry dock on the river. With the growth in tourist traffic, a funicular incline railway and elevators lead to the water's edge and the legendary *Maid of the Mist* cruises to the foot of the falls. Today, the modern *Hornblower Falls* ferries have replaced the aging earlier vessels.

Past Clifton Hill, the historic Queen Victoria Park dominates the landscape. On the river side of the route a pedestrian promenade leads along the stone fence, offering unimpeded views of the waterfalls. Along the way, the small stone Rambler's Rest Pavilion has, since 1907, offered shelter from the rain and mist to strollers.

Curious visitors also crowded here to watch daredevils risk their lives balancing precariously on tightropes which stretched high over the foaming river.

Those who attracted the largest crowds were the tightrope walkers Blondin and Farini. They drew gasps among the throngs when they rode across the tightrope on bicycles, carried a nervous passenger on their back, or crouched to cook an egg on a stove, all while balancing high above the river.

In 2012, Nik Wallenda, a member of the Wallenda family of high-wire artists, balanced his way on a tightrope over the Horseshoe Falls. Millions watched the feat

The historic Queen Victoria Place Restaurant is a busy fine dining establishment in Queen Victoria Park along River Road.

on television. He completed his crossing by somersaulting on the wire. Unlike the others, he was tethered to a safety harness.

Queen Victoria Park

On the opposite side of the road, Queen Victoria Park offers a different kind of viewing experience. Dating from 1885, the walkways begin at the historic gates, pathways wind through the park among hanging baskets, a hybrid tea rose garden and many other floral displays. The paths converge at the historic Niagara Parks Police station, a service which dates to 1887.

Overlooking the grounds near the station house is the statue of King George VI, the grandfather of the current King Charles III. The granite statue was designed by Wyn Wood and carved by Louis Temporale. It commemorates the King's visit to Canada and the United States in 1939. Because he had served in the British Navy during World War I, the statue depicts him wearing the uniform of the First Lord of the Admiralty.

Further south, where Murray Street winds from River Road up the bluff, the Queen Victoria Place Restaurant and Welcome Centre has stood since 1904. Built using boulders gathered from the river, it was

first called the Refectory Restaurant, and features a copper roof. Having also served originally as the residence of the Niagara Parks Commissioner and later housing a popular dance hall, it has been much re-modelled and is now a fine food restaurant.

The path then comes to the building, which projects the brilliant signature light show onto the face of the falls. Falls illumination is not a new feature; it began in 1860 to honour a visit by the Prince of Wales. In 1879, the lights shone forth again to mark the royal visit of Princess Louise and the Marquess of Lorne.

In 1925, lights were permanently installed atop the OPG water surge tank next to the Queen Victoria Place Restaurant. The lighting system has been upgraded several times. The entire operation today is run from a small control panel in an elongated room overlooking the illumination lights. The operator can change the lights by manually turning a series of red, blue, green, and yellow colour coded toggle switches.

Niagara Falls Incline Railway

Leading up the bluff opposite Table Rock is the new Niagara Falls Incline Railway. Such railways have long operated at the falls, dating back more than two centuries, with as many as five on the Canadian side alone.

The new incline railway was constructed in 2013 as a shortcut linking the growing Fallsview district above the bluff with Table Rock House. It replaced a 50-year-old railway. Unlike the earlier version, today's railcars are enclosed.

In 2019, after a pause of 28 years, another incline railway, the Hornblower Funicular Railway resumed operation. The railcars descend the 56-metre cliff from River Road to the Hornblower docks below. Both incline railways operate in pairs with the cars operating on connected cables which counterbalance each other, so that, as one descends, it pulls the other upward.

Queen Victoria Park ends at the incline railway. A statue of Nikola Tesla stands nearby. Tesla was a Croatian scientist who convinced the world that alternating current electricity was more efficient and reliable than Thomas Edison's direct current.

Niagara Parks Power Station

The Niagara Parks Power Station is one of today's major tourist attractions. It stands a short distance from the Table Rock and was completed in 1905. After it was decommissioned, it was acquired by the Niagara Parks Commission. The Commission preserved the turbines and other interior components, opening the facility as a museum in 2021. Sixty metres below the main hall, the curving 700-metre tailrace tunnel, through which the rushing waters exited to the river, was repurposed as a walkway with information plaques lining the corridor.

Within a few paces of the Niagara Parks Power Station is the Floral Display House. Then, a hundred metres further upstream by the river, the impressive Ontario Power Station is a National Historic Site yet to be reopened for visitors.

One of the most popular attractions in Niagara Falls is a trip on the modern *Hornblower* ferry, long known as the *Maid of the Mist*.

The historic stone shelter on the Gorge Walkway has long offered respite from the elements.

Old Scow Lookout Point

From the Old Scow Lookout Point, adjacent to the Ontario Power Station on the bank, visitors can see the river rushing past the rusting relic of a scow stuck fast on a rock.

It has been there since 1918, when, as part of a dredging operation, it broke loose from its tug and hurtled through the rapids towards the brink of the falls with two terrified workers aboard. The quick-thinking workers realized that by flooding the compartments they could slow the barge's progress; it worked as the barge grounded itself on a rock. The question became how to rescue the two workmen.

The United States Coast Guard came to the rescue. They fired a lifeline from a cannon to the vessel and then ran a sling along the rope. The workmen climbed into the sling and were pulled to safely. Or so they thought; partway across the sling stalled. Another rescue came when a noted

The monument to Nikola Tesla shows him standing on one of the generators that captured power from the falls.

local river man named Red Hill inched his way along the cable out to the frightened pair and, working through the night, untangled the ropes. Finally, the pair scrambled onto solid ground to the cheers of the thousands of onlookers. Information plaques in the Old Scow Lookout Point Park beside the power plant describe the terrifying ordeal.

Time and ice floes have damaged the scow since then, causing parts to tear off and the barge to shift. In 2022, ice caused some movement of the scow. It may yet break loose and tumble over the brink.

SLEEPING OVER
Modern and Historic Hotels

Niagara Falls has long been billed as the Honeymoon Capital of the World. The nickname originated in the early 1800s after Napoleon's brother, Jérôme-Napoléon Bonaparte, spent his honeymoon there and returned home with glowing reports. Since virtually everyone emulated royalty in that era, and still do, the place gained a reputation as a newlywed haven.

The first hotels to appear at Niagara Falls were the famous Pavilion Hotel, the Ontario House, the Canada House and Wilson's Tavern.

Wilson's Tavern was owned and operated by Charles Wilson. He purchased 100 hectares of land and in 1797 he built his tavern along Portage Road overlooking the falls. In 1817, William Forsyth bought the tavern and renamed it Prospect House. It is today the site of Table Rock Centre.

In 1833, the first Clifton Hotel was built at the base of Ferry Road (Clifton Hill) by Harmanus Crysler. This large hotel was considered the best hotel available and the flagship of all Niagara hotels to follow.

Niagara's Fallsview Casino area stands high atop a post-glacial river bluff.

The Old Stone Inn is a new boutique hotel constructed around the walls of an historic mill.

The railway began bringing more visitors in the 1850s. By 1855, seven more hotels had appeared, most of them located on Bridge Street across from the station. By 1930, more than a dozen hotels had appeared on the streets of Niagara Falls.

It is no surprise that the auto age ushered in a surge in accommodation, this time in the form of motels with parking essentially right at the front door of the rooms. Many motels still appear along the streets of Niagara Falls. At the same time, train travel dwindled and the station hotels closed. Only the Hotel Europa still stands opposite the old station, with its windows boarded up. The Europa opened in 1910 and contained 40 rooms, a nightclub and restaurant. It closed in the early 2000s.

New modern chain hotels have located on River Road along with attractive B&Bs, many of which are in the historic homes that line the road.

Fallsview District Inns and Hotels

The casino boom opened a new area for accommodation. The Fallsview district along Stanley Avenue near Murray Street hosts the 53-storey Hilton Fallsview Hotel and Resort, with 1,000 rooms, casino, nightclub and spa as well as the 432-room Marriot. Other hotels cluster nearby, including the Embassy Suites, the Oakes Hotel and the Days Inn. More than 40 motels, hotels, and inns now make Niagara Falls one the most well-equipped accommodation centres in Ontario.

General Brock Hotel

On July 1, 1929, the General Brock Hotel, located on Falls Avenue, was officially opened. At 11 storeys, it was the tallest building in the city or anywhere in Niagara for that matter. The hotel boasted 247 bedrooms, 290 telephones and two elevators.

The Brock Hotel was considered the first skyscraper and luxury hotel in Niagara. It attracted such celebrities as Walt Disney, Shirley Temple, and Jimmy Stewart. In 1952, the luxury suites became home to Marilyn Monroe while filming her classic noir film, *Niagara*. The hotel appeared on film at the ending of *The Whole Nine Yards* starring Matthew Perry. The scene was filmed on the balcony terrace on the 11th floor.

The hotel has changed names over the years, and is currently the Crown Plaza Hotel.

Old Stone Inn

Another hotel with much history is the Old Stone Inn. It is located in the centre of Niagara Falls, halfway between Clifton Hill and the Fallsview district.

The original portion of the building dates from 1904, when it served as a flour mill. In 1977 it was repurposed as a boutique hotel. New additions now engulf the mill portion although those stone walls

The interior of The Old Stone Inn has retained the stone wall from the early mill.

remain visible within the hotel. The renovations have stayed true to its 1904 roots with a historic architectural design that includes those rugged stone walls, along with wooden beams, barn boards and cobblestone flooring. The inn is noted for its Scratch Kitchen restaurant with fresh produce.

Sterling Inn

It was milk that made the Sterling Inn what it is today, a dairy that has been repurposed into one of Niagara's newest boutique hotels and B&B. Located at 5195 Magdalen Street, close to Clifton Hill, the dairy was opened in 1928 by Fred Cairns and purchased by Borden's Dairy in 1930.

For 44 years the dairy and creamery were a landmark in Niagara Falls, noted especially for its fresh bottled milk and ice cream. Borden's operated the dairy until 1974. In 2007, the building became the Sterling Inn and Spa. The building is still easily identified by the giant concrete milk bottle above the main entrance.

Olde Angel Inn

Hotels in Niagara-on-the-Lake date to the 1790s when Loyalists began arriving in the Niagara Peninsula.

When Niagara-on-the-Lake, then known as Newark, was designated as the capital of Upper Canada, more rooms for government officials and military personnel were built along the streets. In 1813, the American troops razed most of the community. But

The Pillar and Post Hotel was constructed within a building that formerly housed a cannery.

rebuilding began almost immediately after the war's end, and so many of the historic hotels date to the decades following the end of hostilities.

Among the oldest of the inns is the Olde Angel Inn. Its story dates to 1789, when it was built as the Harmonious Coach House. Badly damaged in the War of 1812, it was rebuilt in 1815, as the Angel Inn. It remains the town's oldest inn and is now called the Olde Angel Inn. It is situated behind the Court House facing what was originally the Market Square.

The Old Bank House Inn was built in 1817 as the first branch of the Bank of Upper Canada and later the Commercial Historic Country Inn. In 1902 the inn hosted the Prince and Princess of Wales. In 2005, by then called the Old Bank House Inn, it hosted Prince Alexander and Princess Katherine of Yugoslavia. The inn now offers nine modernized luxury suites whose guests can enjoy the view of the river from its 50-foot front porch.

The Appletree Inn dates to 1820 when it was built by James Jones. Now a B&B it is located at 263 Regent Street overlooking the Niagara River.

The Moffat Inn, a Georgian vernacular building constructed in 1835, served as a popular local tavern and inn. Built by Richard Moffat, it later housed shops and various offices until 1983, when it was acquired by Morgan and Julie Jones, who repurposed the building as an inn. The façade of the inn is highlighted by a central doorway flanked by two windows with a range of five windows along the second storey. The inn is located at 60 Picton Street.

Having been built as a country home in 1824 by Captain Duncan Milloy of Oban, Scotland, the Oban Inn was considered Niagara's oldest inn. It remained a popular destination until 1993 when a fire destroyed all but the foundation. It was quickly rebuilt exactly as it was and is now a designated heritage location. Transformed again in 2006, the inn offers 26 rooms and lush English gardens. It is located at 160 Front Street opposite the golf course.

Pillar and Post Hotel

The Pillar and Post was built in the 1890s as a cannery, when vegetable and fruit growing was a booming business. That function remained until 1957 when the cannery closed. The building reopened in the 1970s, this time as a restaurant, and then four years later as a 25-room hotel. That capacity has expanded to more than 90 rooms today. The walls of the original canning plant remain visible within the new structure.

Prince of Wales Hotel

The most prominent of the town's heritage hotels is the Prince of Wales. With its towered entrance, it dominates the main intersection of the town at Picton and Queen Streets. The building was originally constructed in 1864 as Long's Hotel, but in 1901, following a visit by the Prince of Wales (later Edward VII), the name was changed to honour the royal visitor. The 110-room luxury hotel has undergone a number of renovations and expansions since then and in 1973 hosted Queen Elizabeth II.

The town is replete with many other B&Bs and smaller inns. In fact, the entire town is a heritage museum piece with its forts, historic main street, Black heritage sites and the popular Shaw Festival.

Niagara-on-the-Lake's Prince of Wales Hotel is an iconic landmark in the town's downtown core.

DOWNTOWN NIAGARA

Historic Main Streets to Explore

Main Street has historically been the heart of Ontario's towns and villages. Each main street offered its own distinct landscape of shops, theatres, town halls and business blocks.

But the automobile, suburban malls and big box stores have killed or reduced many of these historic main streets, leaving the older downtown cores to struggle for survival. Many have succeeded by repurposing their brand, beautifying their walkways, and promoting themselves as the town's historic section.

Other once-prosperous main streets have been left to resemble ghost towns. Niagara has a bit of both.

NIAGARA-ON-THE-LAKE

Situated at the estuary of the Niagara River, the village was founded in 1782 by United Empire Loyalist Isaac Dolson and originally named Butlersburg. Robert Hamilton established a successful merchant business here in 1788. In 1792, the Lieutenant-Governor of Upper Canada, John Graves Simcoe stationed the Queen's Own Rangers

A ride in a vintage carriage, like this one passing the historic Niagara Apothecary, is a popular way to explore downtown Niagara-on-the-Lake.

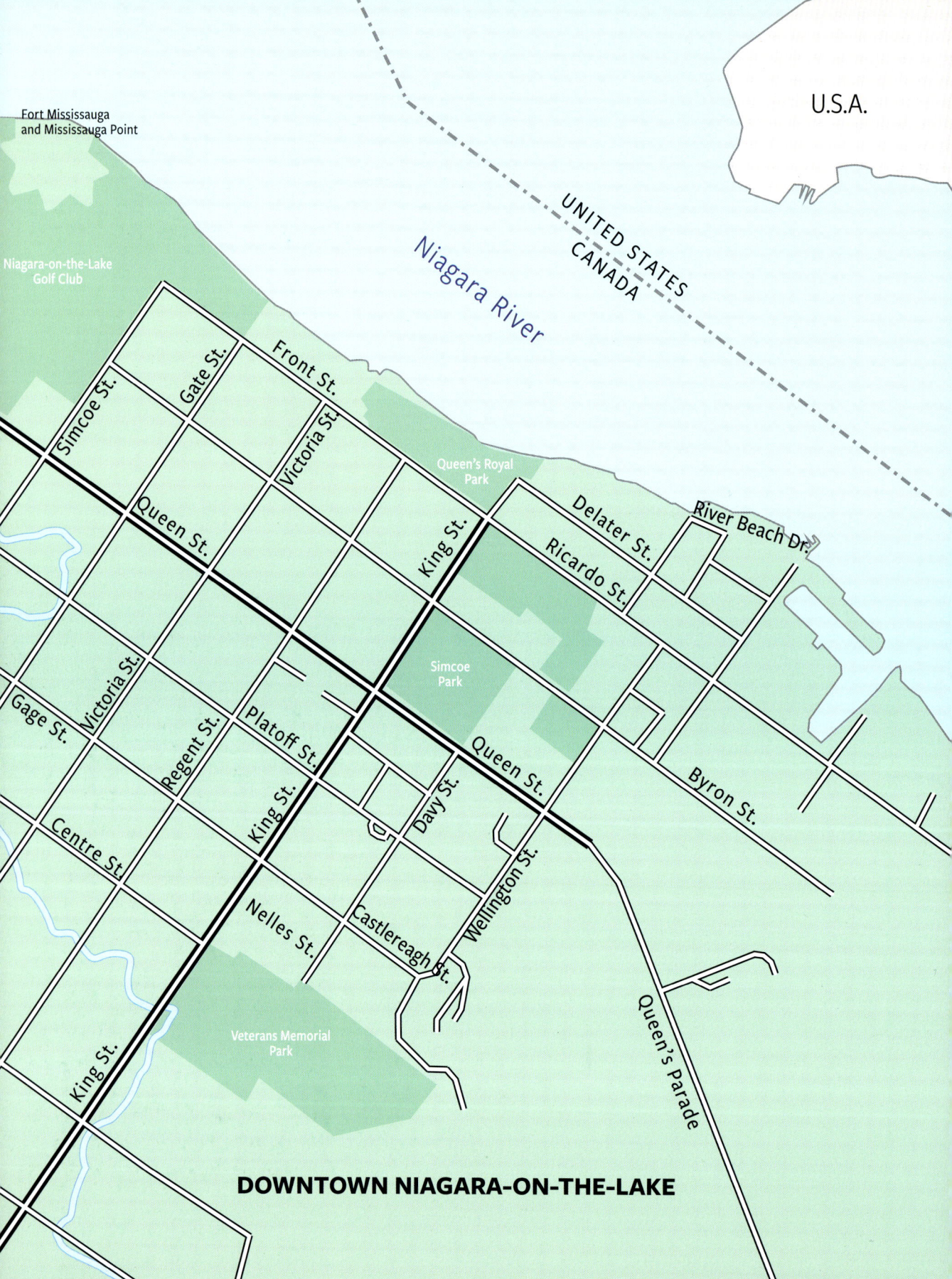

Beautifully preserved heritage buildings in Niagara-on-the-Lake surround what was originally the town square.

here and designated the place as the capital of Upper Canada with the name Newark. Leery of its location opposite the American arsenal at Fort Niagara on the opposite side of the river, in 1796, he relocated the legislature to York (later called Toronto) with its more protected harbour.

By 1802, Niagara was still an important point for shipping and had a ferry service to Lewiston on the opposite shore of the Niagara River. The town contained a customs house and a post office. After American forces destroyed Newark in 1813, the town began to rebuild. Many of today's heritage structures date from the decades following the American retreat. It resumed its role as a major shipping centre importing the goods necessary for its growing environs. In 1847 the building of a county courthouse to serve the counties of Lincoln and Welland added to its importance.

But the heady days did not last. With the opening of a newer and expanded Welland Canal in 1851, the shipping trade moved to Port Dalhousie and Niagara's growth stagnated. In 1862, the county seat was moved to St. Catharines and the grand courthouse

The Olde Angel Inn is one of the oldest and most popular inns in Niagara-on-the-Lake.

building was downgraded to the status of a town hall.

Still, even then, Niagara, as it was then called, was beginning to attract a tourist trade drawn to its bucolic lakeside setting. Catering to the growing numbers of visitors, hotels such as the Queen's Royal Hotel and Long's Hotel (later the Prince of Wales Hotel) sprang up.

Gradually, the town's commerce began to focus on Queen Street. Since the main rail lines, except for a branch line, had bypassed the town, the business district remained small and experienced limited growth. And for today's visitors, that was a good thing. Instead of being overwhelmed by cookie-cutter storefronts, the town is now considered a museum of historic homes and shops and is promoted as such.

A stroll through the historic core shows

how successful that has been. With the opening of the Shaw Festival in the old courthouse (later the Court House Theatre) in the 1960s, restaurants and boutiques began to open and flourish, many adopting historically themed architecture. Each year gardeners cultivate 240 hanging baskets, 100 flower beds and 125 planters.

Prince of Wales Hotel

Dominating the corner of King and Queen Streets stands the Prince of Wales Hotel (so named following a visit by Edward, Prince of Wales, in 1901), with the refurbished Michigan Central Station across the road. The historic Niagara Apothecary, refurbished as an 1860s era drugstore museum, had originally been built in 1820.

The former Court House Theatre sits at Queen Street's mid-block. Dominating the view of the street is the Memorial Clock Tower built to commemorate the fallen soldiers of World War I. Unveiled in 1922, the tower was designed by Toronto architect Charles M. Wilmott and built at a cost of $8,000.

Olde Angel Inn

The one-time market square behind the courthouse is enclosed by historic buildings, including the Olde Angel Inn, which dates from 1789. Within the square, the tourist office is housed in what was once the county gaol. Walking tour guides to the many heritage buildings locations are available here. Most of the heritage sites lie within a few blocks of the town's historic main street. Queen Street remains one of Ontario's most authentically preserved main streets.

The Memorial Clock tower dominates the main street.

QUEENSTON

Described in 1807 as a "neat and flourishing place," Queenston was by then a major centre with 100 dwellings and a population of more than 300.

In 1839, Ontario's first railway opened between Chippawa and Queenston, a horse-drawn tram which ran on wooden rails. The rail line was later upgraded to steam and extended to Niagara (as Niagara-on-the-Lake was then called). In 1893, the tracks of a tourist railway, the Niagara

Port Dalhousie's heritage gaol, with its two cells, once housed sailors and canal workers who engaged in drunken brawls in the local taverns.

Parks and River Railway reached town. But by the 1930s road links began to dominate.

For a number of years Queenston benefited from a bridge link to Lewiston on the opposite American shore. In 1851, the first Queenston-Lewiston suspension bridge opened to wagon traffic over the river. The Ancaster Road (now the York Road, or Regional Road 81) was extended to the crossing. But the new bridge suffered a fate common to many; in 1854 it collapsed into the river. In 1898, it was replaced using the dismantled Falls View Suspension Bridge from Niagara Falls. In 1963, this bridge was dismantled. Today Provincial Highway 405 carries traffic high above the river to Interstate 190 on the American shore. The overgrown section of the Ancaster Road to the site of the one-time bridge and the stone bridge abutments, are all that remain from that earlier bridge.

Although Queenston boasts historic sites like the Laura Secord House and the

DOWNTOWN QUEENSTON

The historic Quebec Bank in downtown Thorold is one of the area's oldest bank buildings and part of the town's main street heritage.

William Lyon Mackenzie printing shop, it lacks the wealth of heritage main street buildings that Niagara-on-the-Lake enjoys. But along its quiet and shady streets, there are a few.

South Landing Inn

The South Landing Inn at 21 Front Street is one such place, dating from 1827. Homes at 48 and 53 Queenston Street and 25 Princess Street also date from the 1820s. In 1834, Robert Hamilton created one of Niagara's grandest homes, Willowbank. Overlooking the village and the river from a high bank, this three-and-a-half storey classic revival mansion resembles more a southern plantation-style home with its prominent pillars. The house is a municipally designated heritage property and a National Historic Site of Canada. Today it houses the School of Restoration Arts.

WELLAND CANAL — PORT DALHOUSIE

By the time the Erie Canal opened across New York State to Buffalo in 1824, the benefits of an all-Canadian canal transportation route were beginning to dawn on Canadians. Unlike the Erie route, however, a possible route in Canada from Lake Ontario to Lake Erie faced an enormous obstacle, the soaring cliffs of the Niagara Escarpment.

In 1824, sod was turned for the new canal in the village of Allanburg, and by 1828, the first schooners entered by way of Twelve Mile Creek at Port Dalhousie. The first canal extended from Port Dalhousie to Port Robinson and then by way of the Welland River to Chippawa on the Niagara River.

Three years later, the canal was extended to Port Colborne on Lake Erie itself. The canal incorporated 42 separate locks. As Port Dalhousie prospered, beside the locks of the canal a boomtown of hotels, bars, and taverns sprang up.

As ships grew larger, so did the canal. The second canal simply followed the route of the first canal, with upgrades to the locks, and was completed in 1845, with new gates installed at Port Dalhousie. A third canal was finished in 1887, but followed a more direct path. From Port Dalhousie it now ran straight to Allanburg, the canal's birthplace.

Welland's main street is noted for its many murals depicting the city's transportation heritage. This one is entitled, *Upbound at Midnight*.

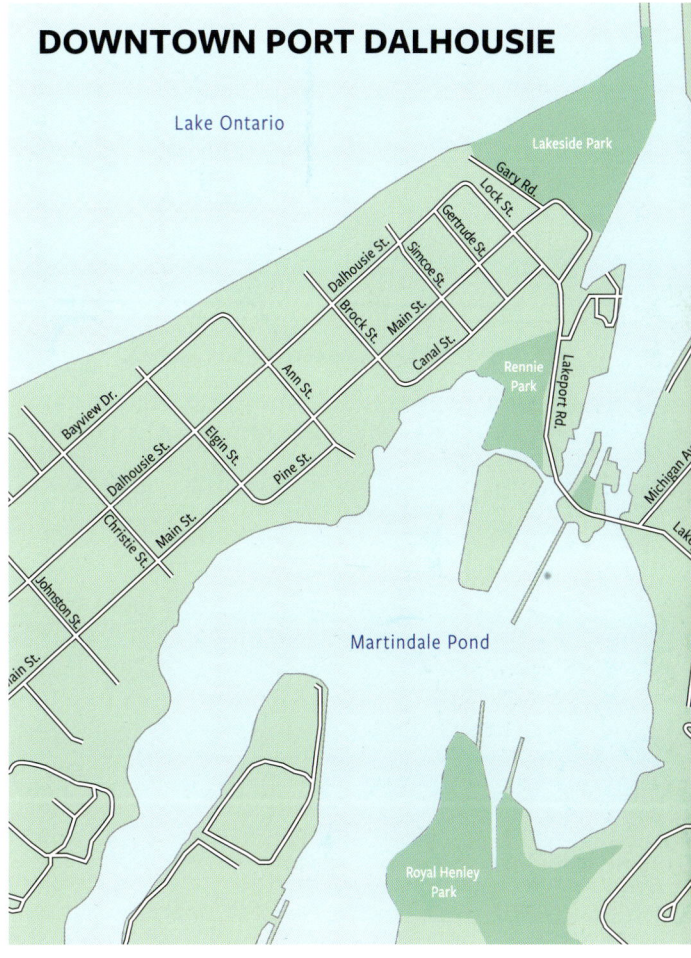

Fourth Welland Canal

A fourth canal changed things significantly. A new port of entry from Lake Ontario was constructed at Port Weller, some distance east of old Port Dalhousie. The fourth canal abandoned Port Dalhousie, and the prosperity of the main street from the canal traffic ended. Up until the 1950s, it did revive as a recreational destination. Summer visitors disembarked from CN cruise ships like the *Cayuga* to enjoy a day in the popular Lakeshore Park with ice cream and a ride on the carousel (hopefully not in that order). The annual Henley Regatta became a major draw as well. Then in 1951, following the tragic fire on the CN cruise ship *Noronic* in Toronto Harbour, CN ceased its cruise excursions. However, with the new QEW and the increase in automobile traffic, the town rebounded as did the little main street.

Olde Lock One Commons

The main streets of the port are short, extending along Lock Street and Lakeport Road. Lock Street today displays a row of historic commercial structures, including

The stone gates at the entrance to Tennessee Avenue in Port Colborne are now a designated heritage site.

the Lock Street Brewing Company. The street meets Lakeport Road, where another historic row of early buildings line the road opposite, along with the preserved Lock Number 1 of the second canal. It is now known as the Olde Lock One Commons.

As Lockport swings around beside the large marina, it passes one of Ontario's smallest gaols. The gaol came in handy as sailors and tow boys would often enjoy a few fisticuffs after a night of imbibing. A short distance away, facing the large parking lot, the famous carousel awaits its summer users, and still costs only a nickel a ride.

Lock Street continues across the Olde Lock One Commons passing the Harbour Club condo development. As the road curves past the condos, it crosses the site of the third canal's Number 1 Lock. Lock 1 today marks the Harbour Walkway Trail in Howes Park with a preserved example of a small white harbour master's cabin.

PORT COLBORNE

Although Port Colborne is the bookend of the canal to Port Dalhousie, the two main streets could not be more different. While the latter is a smaller thoroughfare and more geared to the tourist trade, West Street in Port Colborne is a more traditional main street. As in Port Dalhousie, this main street, known as West Street, developed facing the canal.

The port grew into a significant industrial location. In 1916, the International Nickel Company of Canada (INCO) erected a nickel refinery to the east of the harbour and laid out a townsite of its own. Grain elevators were a key component of the town's industry, with Robin Hood Flour upstream from the lake still sporting its iconic logo on its silos. Grain elevators rise at the mouth of the harbour.

Historic West Street

As the economy of Port Colborne expanded, so did the businesses along West Street. While most of the shops display rather typical small-town architectural styles, one in particular stands out from the rest. Built in 1911, the Imperial Bank of Canada displays a white terra-cotta exterior in the Beaux-Arts style.

Other historic buildings are found here as well. The LG Carter general store at number 230 dates from 1851, while the former Lakeview Hotel at number 62 predates the general store and was built in 1840. At the intersection of West Street and Park Street the former CN train station now serves in part as a restaurant.

Shoppers on West Street may enjoy a stroll along a landscaped walkway beside the canal while watching the mighty lake and ocean vessels lumber their way under the bridge to or from Lock Number 8 just beyond. This lock was constructed not to raise or lower the ships, but rather to control the water levels between the lake and the canal.

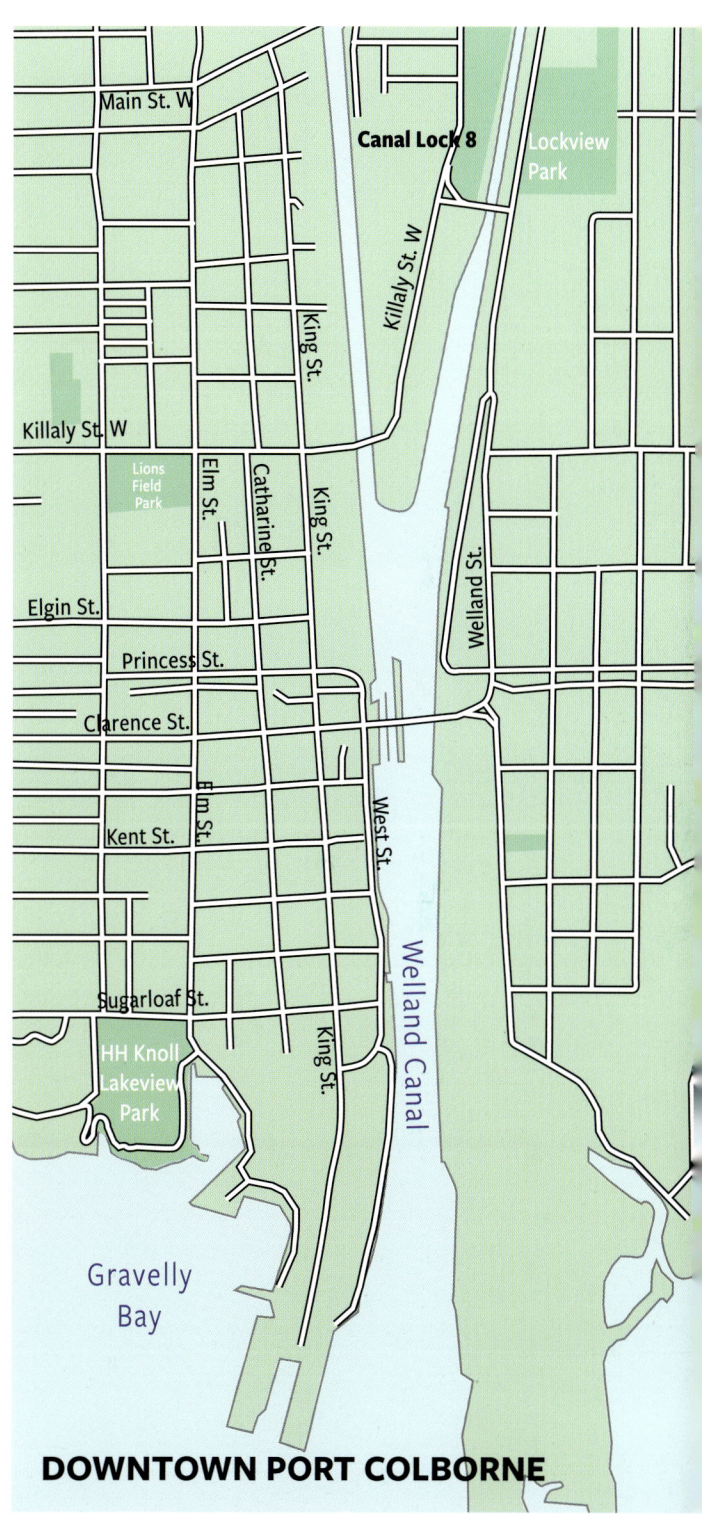

DOWNTOWN PORT COLBORNE

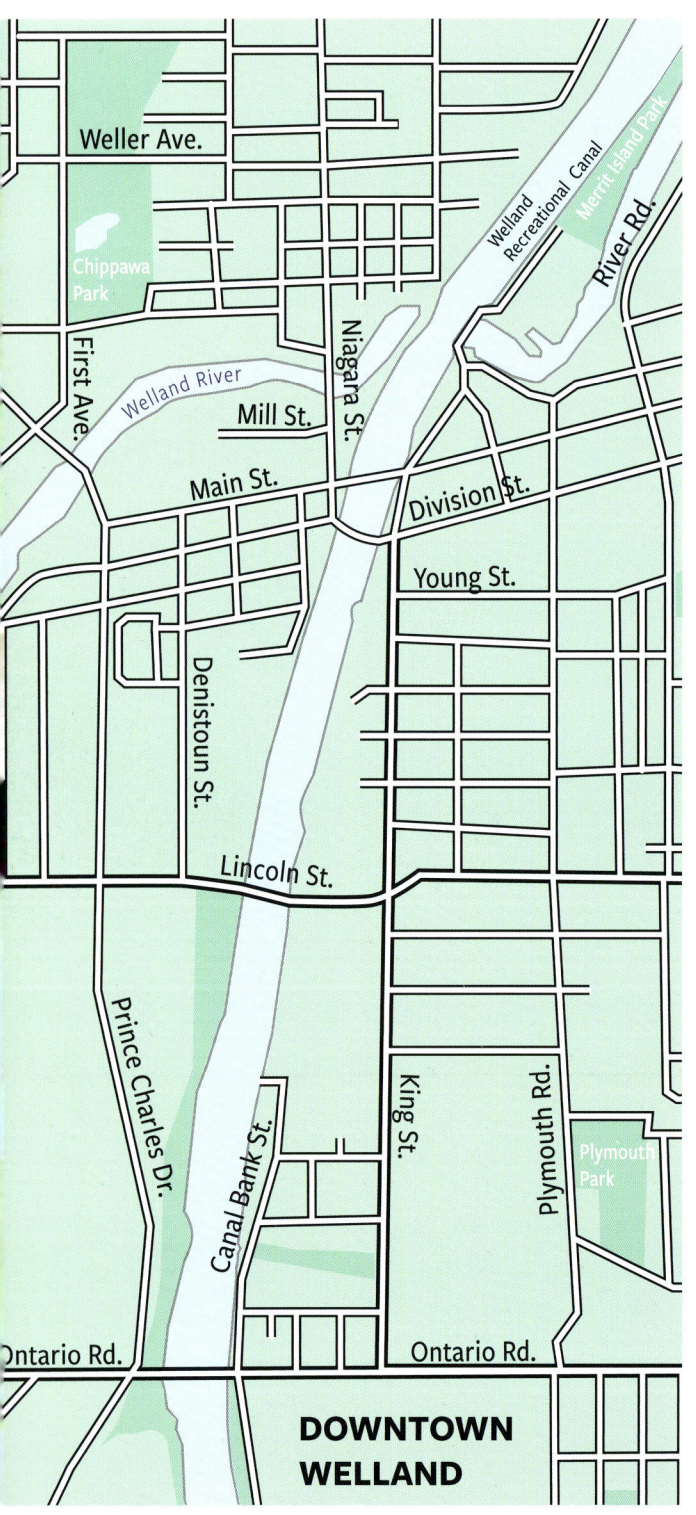

Away from West Street, a few of the residential streets display grand homes under the shade trees on King Street, Caithness, and Fielding Avenue. One of the oddest residential streets is Tennessee Avenue, where wealthy American vacationers from the southern states in 1888 blocked off a stretch of the sandy shoreline to create their private gated enclave they called Solid Comfort. These grand summer homes were secreted behind a set of handsome stone gates to keep out non-members. The residents could even disembark from the trains at their own exclusive station on the railway.

Many new homes now intermingle with the old, including the casino with its multiple hip and gable roofs. And those stone gates have been designated a historical site.

WELLAND

As in so many other small towns, the growth of suburban sprawl and big-box stores drew shoppers away from Welland's downtown core. The city decided it needed to do something to lure shoppers and tourists back to the main street.

In 1986, the city commissioned muralists from across Canada to decorate the exteriors of the buildings throughout the core area with giant murals depicting the city's canal heritage. Today they are more than two dozen murals.

Of that number, 20 are primarily along Main Street and Division Street. Along Main Street East are "Education" at 285 Main Street depicting teachers and students based on old photos; "Triathlon" is also

Train Time, one of more than two dozen murals that decorate Welland's downtown.

displayed at 285 Main Street. The stunning "Upbound at Midnight" at 228 Main Street depicts nighttime traffic on the canal. Scenes from the Welland Fair appear on the side of 228 Main Street, where four murals are grouped around a pair of parking lots on both sides of the street.

South of Main Street East at the bridge, King Street murals depict Welland's historic downtown bustle and canal construction, while Division Street, which parallels Main Street, offers murals titled "Welland's World War I Efforts," "New World," "Three Historic Scenes" and "Wagons."

Building styles here are generally rather nondescript. The most impressive is the former Welland County Court House; it stands at the intersection of Main and Cross Street. The Court House, built in 1855-1856, was designed by Kivas Tully, one of Canada's leading architects, in a neoclassical style. Three storeys high, the limestone building's front façade is dominated by four columns that rise from the second storey porch and are flanked by twin staircases. The former jail stands behind the courthouse.

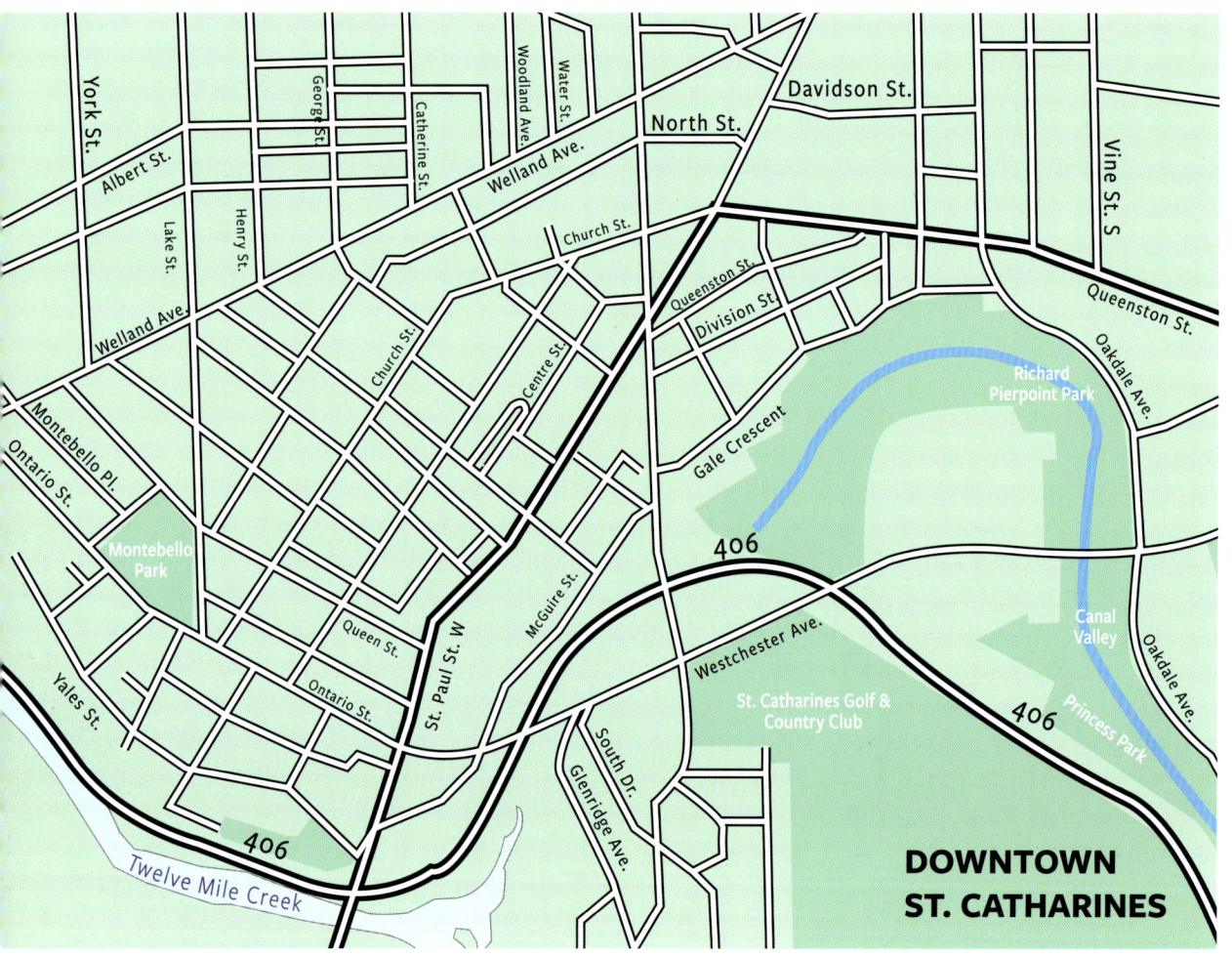

DOWNTOWN ST. CATHARINES

ST. CATHARINES

The influence of the region's Indigenous occupants was instrumental in the shaping of today's St. Catharines, and in particular its historic route through town, St. Paul Street. Their early trails followed Dick's Creek and Twelve Mile Creek and intersected at this point. With the opening of the Welland Canal along Twelve Mile Creek, St. Paul Street which curved along the bank of the creek developed into a busy commercial thoroughfare.

Although the town has lost some important historic structures, including the fine old 1877 Opera House which is now a parking lot, many others have gained new life. These include the 1905 Armoury on Lake Street, now a National Historic Site of Canada. The 1847 Court House and gaol, with its 1863 addition, now house the popular Carousel Players theatre group.

Not all of the downtown heritage rests on St. Paul Street. The Mansion House on William Street dates from the early canal days and is said to be Canada's oldest tavern.

One of the city's most significant buildings is neither its oldest nor its grandest; it is the Salem or Bethel Chapel, which dates from before 1851 and was an important focus for the abolitionist movement in Upper Canada. At the centre of the movement was the resilient Harriet Tubman, known for bravely leading many American slaves to freedom in Canada. This three-level stuccoed structure is also a National Historic Site. It is at the corner of North and Geneva Streets, a few paces from St. Paul.

The St. Catharines Museum initiated a permanent, site-specific installation along St. Paul called History InSite. This initiative juxtaposes historical photographs with modern streetscapes by presenting the photo in, or close to, the place where it was taken. Of the dozen photographs scattered about the city's downtown streets, eight are situated along St. Paul. One study of the more than 70 historic structures along St. Paul confirms that nearly 45 predate 1890.

THOROLD

Another canal-side town, Thorold grew along the eastern bank of the first and second canals. As with many other canal towns, the early main street was named Front Street. The third canal, however, bypassed Thorold, following Ten Mile Creek from Port Weller to Allanburg.

Any evidence of the first canals in downtown Thorold have long disappeared. Front Street, however, has been revitalized and celebrates the town's canal heritage.

Along Front, between Regent Street and

DOWNTOWN THOROLD

Clairmont Street, Thorold has undertaken considerable preservation efforts. An online walking tour leads heritage enthusiasts to the town's 50 designated heritage structures, several of them on Front. These include the Carr-Millar-McMillan Block at 31-35 Front Street. Although the exterior has seen many changes, particularly during the 1940s, the building continues to connect to the streetscape through its scale, business use, and linear connectivity.

A heritage landmark on Albert Street near Front, is the Old Fire Hall. Built in 1876, it dominates the street with it slender bell and hose tower. It is constructed of red brick with yellow brick highlights, including those over the semi-arched windows and the doors.

At 15 Front Street, the MacMillan Drug Store has been a drug store since its construction in 1872. Among its architectural features are the rounded windows on the second floor with stained glass panes. The door case is set off by two squared fluted columns.

Dating from 1853, the Stone Store sits at 11 Front Street. It was constructed by noted stonemason William Martin, using rubble stone. Arched windows look out from the second floor. The adjacent lane-way led to Lock 24 on the second canal, which was located behind the buildings on the street. The building façade has changed little since 1900.

The Quebec Bank, located at 28 Front Street, was built in 1875 for the Canadian Bank of Commerce and then occupied by the Quebec Bank in 1897. It is Canada's second-oldest bank and became Thorold's only bank. Built in the grand Second Empire architectural style, the façade consists of three tall bays. The right-side bay consists of a tall, double-door entry, above which is a semi-elliptical stained-glass window. The eight-foot paired set of panelled doors each have two teardrop rosettes on top, rectangular mouldings in the middle, and two smaller rectangular mouldings at their base.

Built in 1846, the massive limestone Welland Mills is a canal survivor. Other contemporary industrial buildings have been demolished, but Welland Mills is still around, thanks to its heritage value to the town. The four-and-a-half-storey stone building has been a designated heritage property since 1986. At its peak, it was turning out 400 barrels of flour a day. It is situated at 29 Pine Street North adjacent to the downtown.

PORT ROBINSON

Not all towns and villages in Niagara can claim prosperous main streets. Some places are left with what can almost be called ghost main streets. Port Robinson is one of those.

When the waterway first opened in 1828, it was one of the most important places on

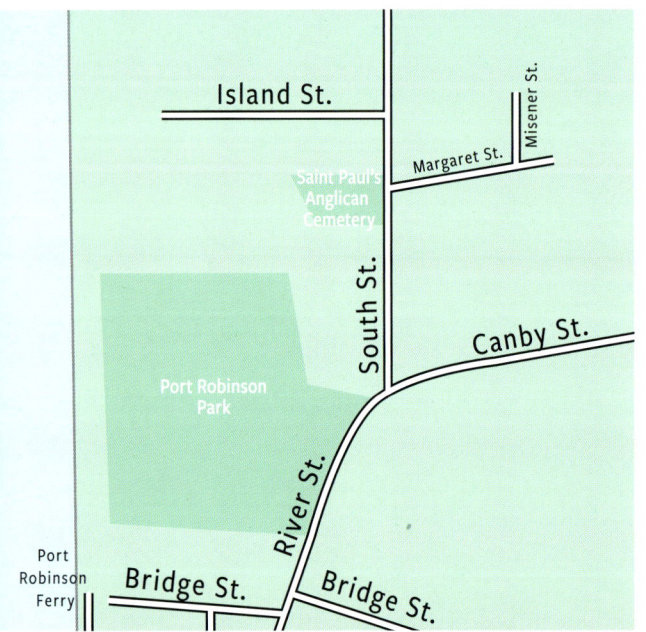

DOWNTOWN PORT ROBINSON

the Welland Canal. During its heyday, Port Robinson could claim a population of 600, along with three busy hotels and a variety of industries, which included a shipyard.

The port gained notoriety in 1974 when a northbound ore carrier, the *Steelton*, crashed into the bridge, totally destroying the structure. It was never replaced, and today only a small passenger ferry links the two sides of the community. Along River Street, the former main street hotels and shops maintain a ghostly presence facing the canal. The name of the Bridge 12 Pub carries on the heritage of that now-vanished bridge. In Port Robinson Park at the north end of the street lie the stone walls of the early lock which linked the canal to the Welland River. A pair of heritage plaques recount the role that the lock played.

Bridge Street leads a few paces to the location of the destroyed bridge, and to where the small boat which takes foot passengers or cyclists to the opposite bank of the canal.

Parallel to the canal, Church Street, basically now just a lane, passes the old lots and foundations of some of the place's vanished earlier businesses. South of the village, the Welland River passes beneath the canal, one of two places along the canal that it does so.

JORDAN VILLAGE

Main streets don't need to be long and grand to provide an interesting stroll. Take, for example, the Village of Jordan on the rim of the scenic valley of Twenty Mile Creek. The earliest settlers were Mennonites from Pennsylvania escaping American persecution following their war for independence. In the valley below, a gristmill ground the local wheat into flour. The village site enjoyed a strategic location, being close to the Queenston Road, an early pioneer trail along the base of the escarpment which linked Queenston with Ancaster.

Produce, including lumber and farm products, was transported to Jordan Harbour and from there shipped to ports

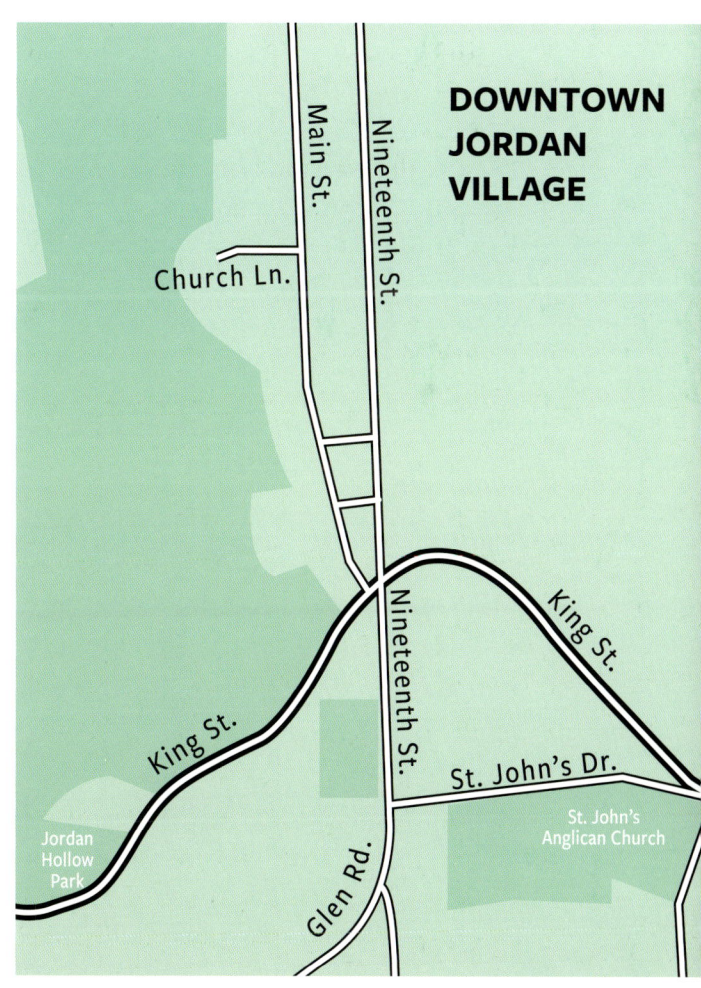

around the west end of the lake. In 1853, the Great Western Railway laid tracks two kilometres to the north of Jordan Village, where a small community called Jordan Station grew beside the tracks. Today, the station, built in 1883, stands authentically preserved on the south side of Prince William Street in Jordan Village.

As tourists began visiting the growing numbers of wineries in the region, Cave Spring Vineyard opened a sales outlet in Jordan Village and the appearance of the main street was dramatically altered. A new string of shops opened on the west side of the street, containing boutiques, an art gallery, and the Cave Spring Cellars, where wine tastings and tours can be enjoyed. The short tree-lined main street which runs south from the shops leads past a string of early homes and one-time hotels.

Along the way, Church Lane leads to the Lincoln Museum and Cultural Centre and one of Ontario's oldest Mennonite meeting houses, the Fry House. The Fry House is a two-storey wooden structure built in 1815 by Mennonite settlers Jacob Fry and Elizabeth Wismer who hailed from Bucks County, Pennsylvania. The Haines Cemetery, with burials dating to the 1840s, is beside it.

The grounds also include an 1859 one-room school from the village which was active until 1948. The building was restored by the Town of Lincoln in 1997 and now offers today's schoolchildren the opportunity to experience a 1908 school curriculum. There is also an access path to the 20 Valley Trail, with steps leading from the museum to the creek.

The Inn on the Twenty, a historic upscale inn, stands at the north end of the main street, while marking the south end is the recently reopened Jordan House Tavern and Lodging.

RIDGEWAY

Located just north of Crystal Beach, the downtown main street of this historic community is also worth a leisurely stroll. The streetscaping has added an allure to the heritage stores which line its sidewalks. The Ridgeway Museum also provides artifacts and insight into the Battle of Ridgeway fought with the Fenian rebels in the 1860s.

NIAGARA FALLS

Queen Street is the historic main street of early Niagara Falls as it grew near the Grand

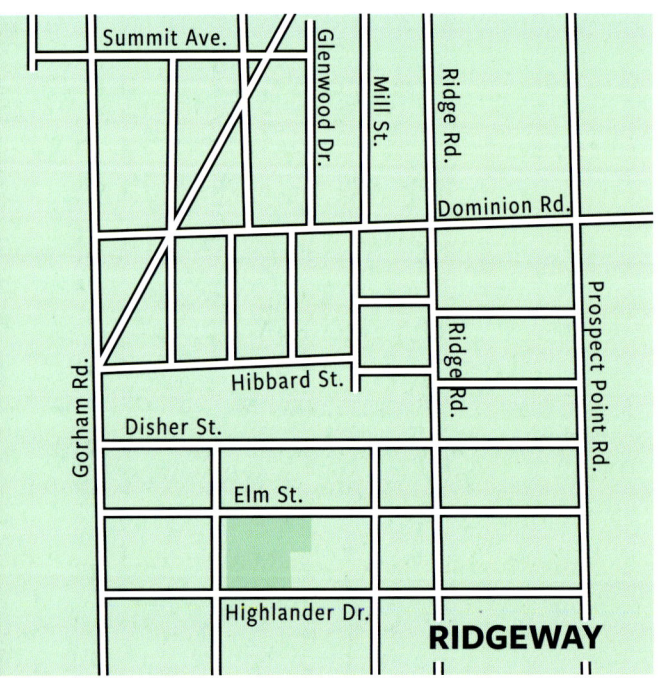

The historic stone former Custom's Building marks the earliest commercial core and dates back to when Niagara Falls was called Clifton.

Trunk Railway station. The street burst into existence with the construction of the international bridge and the arrival of the Great Western Railway in 1853. At first, the town around the Great Western station had taken on the name Elgin. A string of hotels and early functions such as a bank and customs house grew by the depot. Only two of the old hotel buildings remain along Bridge Street, including the large and now-vacant Hotel Europa. As train travel increased, the commercial core shifted and became Queen Street. The area has since been incorporated into the City of Niagara Falls.

The downtown core is marked by decorative arches across Queen Street between Erie and Victoria Streets. Former hotels and the early theatre are among the key heritage structures, as is the elegant stone former customs house located at the corner of Park and Zimmerman Streets. On Zimmerman at Bridge Street, the Old Imperial Bank is another handsome limestone structure. It was designed by architects Darling and Pearson, who were also the designers of Toronto's CP station at Summerhill on Yonge Street in Toronto.

The bank's central location in downtown Niagara Falls made it a significant player in the economic development of the surrounding businesses. As one of the few old commercial structures remaining in the area, the Old Imperial Bank is a remarkable symbol of the once-prosperous village of Elgin.

SILVERTOWN

More a residential community than a commercial main street, this forgotten neighbourhood has a history that is tied to the International Silver Factory which opened here in 1911 and became famous for its Rogers brand of silverware. It was one of several silver-plating foundries there.

A few years prior to the arrival of the factory, a plan of a subdivision was laid out to the north of the adjacent Grand Trunk Railway station and yards. When the plant opened, the workers took up the lots in the subdivision to be close to their jobs and the community became known as Silvertown.

Buttrey Street, an industrial row defining the south side of the neighbourhood, has a few newer industrial uses while the ruins of other industries now lie vacant and overgrown.

Ferguson Street, one block further north, contains today's few commercial buildings. The side streets here resemble little more than laneways. Despite its challenging condition, historical walks occasionally occur, indicating a keen local interest in this historic community and that it is not entirely forgotten.

Factory outlets became a fad in the 1970s when brand-name manufacturers began promoting outlet stores, which offered

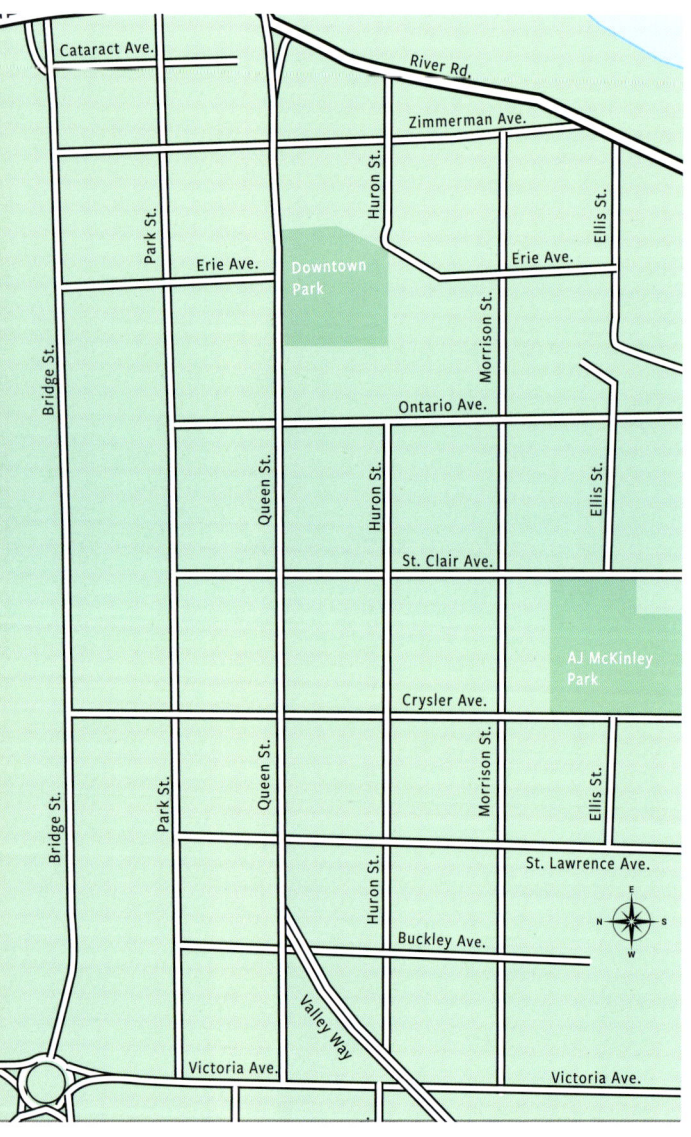

DOWNTOWN NIAGARA FALLS

The entrance to the outlet malls at Niagara Falls, Canada's largest open-air outlet shopping centre.

their products at reduced prices. Since Niagara Falls was a popular destination, Niagara Falls, New York, began to promote outlet shopping and Canadian shoppers came in their cars, vans and by the busload.

Then Niagara Falls, Ontario, decided to get in on the act, and today outlet malls on the Canadian side have become an important component of the Niagara tourism industry.

At 50,000 square metres, the Outlet Collection at Niagara is the area's largest open-air outlet mall. Located just off the QEW at the Glendale Avenue exit, the centre features more than 100 outlet brands, including Aritzia, Tommy Hilfiger Outlet, Kate Spade, Nike Factory Store, Coach, Steve Madden, Lululemon, Under Armour, Polo Ralph Lauren, Marshalls and others.

Meanwhile on Lundy's Lane, Niagara's busiest commercial strip, the Canada One Outlets is one of the road's feature attractions. At Canada One Outlets shoppers can find over 20 outlets, such as Coach, Tommy Hilfiger, Guess, Adidas, American Eagle, SVP Sports, Urban Planet, Urban Kids, Carter's OshKosh, La Vie en Rose, Laura, Suzy Shier, Tootsies Factory Shoe Market, Rocky Mountain Chocolate, Samsonite, to name only a few.

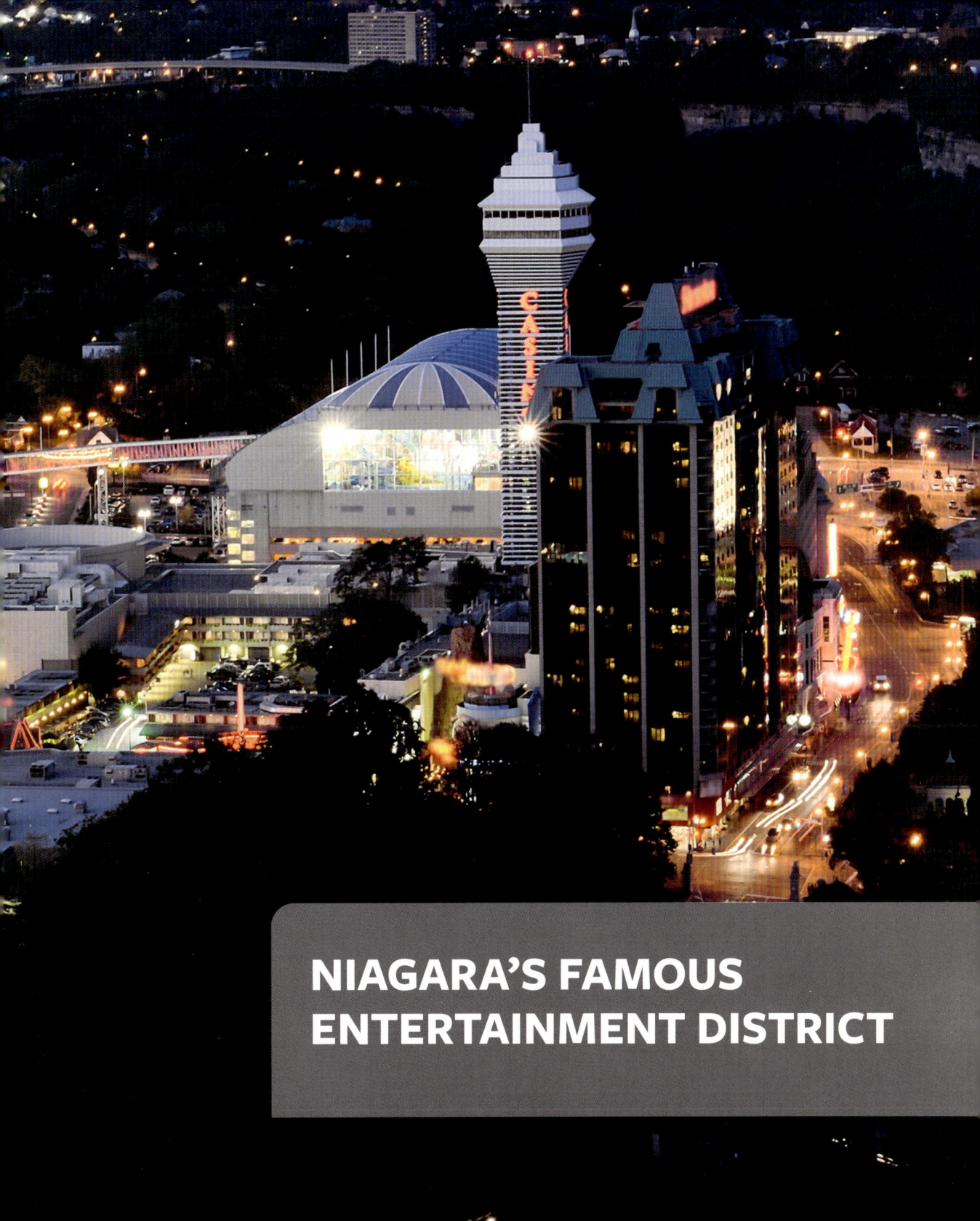

NIAGARA'S FAMOUS ENTERTAINMENT DISTRICT

THAT'S ENTERTAINMENT

Tourism, from the Fractious Front to Midways and Casinos

It didn't take long following the end of hostilities from the War of 1812 for opportunists smelling tourist dollars to flock to the falls. The first on the Canadian side was a questionable character named William Forsyth. The war had scarcely ended when Forsyth was building the Pavilion Inn beside the lip of the waterfall and also building a stairway to the foot of the cascade.

By then, tourists were following what was called the Fashionable Tour. It was an itinerary for wealthy Americans from the southern states who journeyed from South Carolina to Albany, New York, from which point they came by the Erie Canal to Buffalo and on to Niagara.

Others followed Forsyth and erected hotels, taverns, and stairways along the brink of the falls. In 1827, Thomas Barnett built the Table Rock Museum approximately 100 metres south of Table Rock, a rock ledge which projected out from the cliff, and he built a staircase to the base of the falls.

Some of the many tourist attractions on Clifton Hill. Casino Niagara can be seen in the background.

Previous spread: **The Niagara SkyWheel at night.**

Movieland is one of many popular attractions in the area.

Other opportunists soon moved in. Most notable among these was Saul Davis, of Buffalo, New York, who in 1844 built the Prospect House and a few years later the Table Rock House. Vicious competition among the property owners led to a flurry of vandalism, arson and assaults, as well as multiple lawsuits.

In 1831, Harmanus Crysler began construction of the Clifton Hotel, located at the foot of Clifton Hill. It was rebuilt following a fire in 1898 and remained the town's most important hostelry until 1932, when it was replaced with the attractive Oakes Garden.

The Front

Between Clifton House and the Table Rock House, more hucksters flocked to the scene, illegally grabbing up the land which lay in the military reserve along the cliff. As the tourists began to flood in, the road along the rim of the gorge became known as The Front. Here could be found all manner of "touts, blackguards, entrepreneurs and

Dinosaur Adventure Golf with the SkyWheel in the background.

confidence men," as Pierre Berton wrote so colourfully in his book *Niagara*.

Fed up with the reputation which Niagara Falls was getting, the Ontario government created the Niagara Parks Commission in 1883 with a mandate to acquire the Front and create a landscaped garden and a walkway along the brink of the gorge which became Queen Victoria Park and the promenade that remain to this day.

It took the arrival of the railways to really usher in Niagara's tourist era. In 1854, the Great Western Railway built their station north of the falls. In the 1870s, the Canada Southern Railway, which had taken over the Erie and Niagara, added station stops that offered views of the falls.

As tourists flocked to the falls, Clifton Hill began to attract campgrounds and hotels. In the 1950s, Clifton Hill was home to many weird and bizarre attractions. Among the first to open were the Houdini Hall of Fame, the Tussaud Wax Museum and Ripley's Believe It or Not.

One of Clifton Hill's zany new attractions, the Upside Down House, offers visitors a chance to walk on the ceiling as they tour the house.

Canada's Midway

Soon, the attractions began to spill onto the other streets as well. Tourists now flock to the bright lights and sounds of Canada's midway. They come to ride the 53-metre SkyWheel or play on the world's largest mini-golf course, the 70,000-square-foot Dinosaur Adventure Golf, ride the go-carts at the Niagara Speedway or play the 300 interactive games at the Great Canadian Midway. The scares are still there, too: the Screaming Tunnels, Alien Encounter, Dino Rampage, Dracula's Haunted Castle, the Nightmares Fear Factory and the old stand-by, the House of Frankenstein.

Ontario's largest model train layouts and one of Niagara's newest interactive features is Locomoland. On the second floor of what was formerly the Rock Legends Wax Museum, kids and model railway enthusiasts will find a 2,000-square-foot remote-controlled miniature railway system, with trains scooting through four separate areas.

Rail buffs can also experience the view from the engine cab through micro-cameras built into the trains and operate them from remote control stations throughout the display area. This attraction is on Centre Street north of Victoria Avenue.

Niagara's Casinos

Long before the arrival of Europeans on the Atlantic shores, forms of gambling were common among Indigenous people. Before 1892, gambling remained unregulated in Canada, but in that year, the newly enacted Criminal Code outlawed all forms of gambling.

In 1925, the Code was amended to allow gambling at local fairs. In 1969, another amendment permitted lotteries. Finally, in 1985, the federal Criminal Code was amended to allow each province to enact its own gambling laws. Casinos became legal, and Canada's first casino opened in Winnipeg in 1985. It was followed by Caesar's Casino in Windsor in 1994.

In 1996, Casino Niagara opened on the former site of the Maple Leaf Village at Clifton Hill, offering 1,400 slot machines and 40 table games. Today, it offers gamblers 2,400 slot machines and 79 gaming tables spread over 10,000 square metres on three floors.

The Casino and Skylon Towers

While the casino is a recent structure, the Oneida Tower beside it dates to the Maple Leaf Village days. Designed by architect

The Niagara Falls casino tower with the Hard Rock Cafe in front.

Alan Moody, the 120-metre tower opened in 1965 as part of the Maple Leaf Village shopping complex.

The tower originally served as an observation tower which could accommodate 1,600 patrons each hour. The 50-second-long elevator ride would take passengers 82 metres to the lower observation level. From this lower deck, viewers could walk up to the top observation deck located three metres above. The upper deck was partially open air, providing excellent—if vertiginous—views of the falls. Openings in the wire mesh fencing allowed for unimpeded photographs.

Now known as the Casino Tower, it no longer allows public access, serving solely as a landmark for the casino. The Casino entrance is located on Falls Avenue.

Now, of course, there is a higher tower, the Skylon Tower. Construction on it began in May 1964, and was officially opened on October 6, 1965. The Tower offers three observation decks, including an indoor/outdoor deck and two dining rooms. The total height of the tower from the base to the top of the flashing beacon is 160 metres. Three elevators speed visitors to the top in just 52 seconds. Vistas from the observation decks extend to Lake Erie and Lake Ontario, as well as providing an unparalleled overview of the falls and gorge.

In 2004, the Fallsview Casino, with its resort and nightclub acts, turned Canada's honeymoon capital into a mini-Las Vegas. In 2022, the casino added the 5,000 seat OLG Stage concert hall, where the popular

Niagara Falls Casino and Resorts at sunset.

Fallsview's Teslatron display is decorated for Christmas.

This building on Port Colborne's Tennessee Avenue was formerly called a casino, an early name for a dance hall.

Canada's Got Talent television show was staged. A more intimate concert venue is Fallsview's 1,500 seat Avalon Theatre. Overall, the facility offers visitors 3,500 slot machines and more than 100 gaming tables.

Aside from its gambling halls, the resort also includes 18 restaurants, a 30-shop Galleria, a spa, and 372 hotel rooms. The resort was designed by architect Eberhard Zeidler in what is known as the Belle Époque style, popular in Victorian England. Marking the entrance drive, a fountain dances in changing coloured lighting, reminiscent of the light show at the falls itself.

The lights and the buzz of the Fallsview Casino Resort are located at the intersection of Murray Street and Fallsview Boulevard, and along with the other new hotels, resembles a miniature version of the famous gambling strip in Las Vegas.

Fort Erie Race Track

Casinos aren't the only place to gamble. There is also the risk and excitement of a horse race nearby.

On June 16, 1897, the Fort Erie Jockey Club ran its first races at a new facility called the Fort Erie Race Track. Following World War I, the government of Ontario decided to ban fun. Just as prohibition was on the horizon, the province imposed a more onerous tax policy on the race track which reduced the amount of racing that the track could offer.

In 1959, influential horse racing magnate and political influencer E.P. Taylor introduced the Canadian Triple Crown of

Racing which included the prized Prince of Wales Stakes. The Fort Erie Race Track now hosts the second leg of the Triple Crown. The other two legs of the Canadian Triple Crown are the King's Plate at the Woodbine Race Track in Toronto and the Breeders' Stakes on the E.P. Taylor Turf Course, also at Woodbine.

In 1972, the Fort Erie Race Track introduced computerized betting. In 1996, the Ontario government opened the door for gambling at Ontario's race tracks in addition to betting on the horses. On September 11, 1999, a casino area at Fort Erie was opened, featuring 1,200 slot machines. Results of the races can now also be viewed via a new control room with graphic and electronic photo-finish capabilities.

Many famous horses began their storied careers at the Fort Erie track, the most noteworthy being Northern Dancer, who, in 1963, won the first of seven races before going on to wider fame.

Fort Erie Race Track's centerpiece is its beautiful infield, filled with flowers and scenic ponds. In 1961, a horse named Puss n Boots couldn't resist the water and decided to take a detour and enjoy a refreshing dip in the ponds, despite leading the race at the top of the stretch.

This historic racetrack lies along Catherine Street, a short distance west of Concession Road in the west end of Fort Erie.

Great Wolf Lodge

Not only does Niagara have its own mini-Las Vegas, it also has a Disney-style resort. That feature is Great Wolf Lodge Water Park Resort. The Lodge opened its doors in 2006, the first of the chain to operate in Canada and the seventh Great Wolf Lodge worldwide. Amenities include an elaborately themed water park, a spa, and hot tubs. There are grills, buffets and pizza restaurants, as well as a bar, a cafe, a coffee shop and a poolside eatery.

Like Disney resorts, it is mostly for families with young children. It has its own cast of cartoon characters, known as the Great Wolf Kids, 11 anthropomorphic animal characters with names like Wiley Wolf, Brinley Bear, Sammy Squirrel, and Specs the Owl. They are the featured cast in an animated movie called *The Great Wolf Pack: A Call to Adventure.*

Great Wolf Lodge also features an activity game called MagiQuest, a games arcade, and Great Wolf Stuffing Station where kids can create their own stuffed toys. Ten Paw Alley is a kid-sized bowling alley and there is a miniature golf course. Youngsters can learn about the environment from a show with talking animals called the Forest Friends Show. While the children are taking in the junior attractions, parents may avail themselves of the gym or spa.

Among the more than 350 units of accommodation are cabins and themed suites some of which include lofts, fireplaces and breakfast nooks. Day visits are available as well. Great Wolf Lodge is situated on Victoria Avenue close to the Niagara River Parkway.

Great Wolf Lodge in Niagara Falls echoes theme resorts such as those at Disneyworld.

WORLD-CLASS THEATRE AND VINEYARDS

THE PLAY'S THE THING

The Shaw Festival and the Arts

Much of the early entertainment in Niagara took place in theatres. Before radio and television were available in every Ontario home, families seeking entertainment would head to the local theatres to take in a vaudeville act. These acts provided entertainment ranging from variety sketches to comedy routines, short plays, songs, dances, acrobatics, magic shows, trained animal acts and, eventually, they introduced some of the province's first moving pictures.

Moving pictures began to gain attention as early as the 1890s. Most were mini-travelogues and moved from venue to venue and from town to town. Moving pictures gradually became full-fledged stories and before too long, theatres and stores began to be repurposed as permanent movie venues. Then purpose-built theatres began to appear on Ontario's main streets. These were ideal in an age when many patrons could simply walk a few blocks from home to take in the latest Hollywood blockbusters.

With the arrival of the automobile age in the 1950s, theatres realized they needed parking lots and moved to the suburbs and the downtown theatres began to close. St. Catharines alone had four within a few blocks on or near St. Paul Street; all are gone.

A statue of playwright George Bernard Shaw near the Shaw Festival Theatre in Niagara-on-the-Lake.

The Royal George Theatre at 85 Queen Street in Niagara-on-the-Lake was one which did survive. It was built originally as a vaudeville house to entertain troops during World War I. In the 1950s, it operated as a movie theatre. It has been restored and is now offering live theatre during the annual Shaw Festival.

Another movie house survivor stands in Niagara Falls' historic downtown at 4624 Queen Street. Built in 1941, the Seneca Queen Theatre, known simply as the Seneca, was designed by renowned architect Jay English. The theatre was noted for hosting the premier of the classic Marilyn Monroe film, *Niagara*.

Today, Niagara Falls offers visitors the Greg Frewin Theatre at 5781 Ellen Avenue for dinner, dancing and magic shows. The Casino District on Stanley Avenue includes the OLG Stage and the Avalon Theatre in the Fallsview Casino. Audiences can reminisce with long-established legends of music such as Billy Joel, Chubby Checker, Barry Manilow and Paul Anka.

Shaw Festival

Happily, live theatre is far from dead. Following the success of the Stratford Shakespearian Festival in the early 1950s, the Shaw Festival in Niagara-on-the-Lake opened its inaugural season on June 29, 1962, in the assembly room of the old courthouse on the main street of Niagara-on-the-Lake. The festival's early promoters were Calvin Rand of Buffalo and Brian Dohery of Niagara-on-the-Lake.

Then, on June 28, 1973, Queen Elizabeth II rolled up in a limousine to officially open

a new Festival Theatre. The internationally acclaimed venue, designed by Ronald Thom, permitted larger audiences and an expended repertoire. Now, the festival can offer more than a dozen productions during

The Royal George Theatre in Niagara-on-the-Lake, once a vaudeville venue, is now a key site of the town's popular annual Shaw Festival.

the season, which runs from February to December. It has expanded its repertoire to include works that were written during Shaw's lifetime, as well as those written by Shaw himself.

In 1980, the festival acquired the Royal George Theatre, transforming it from a movie theatre into a miniature version of an Edwardian opera house. The festival also opened the Jackie Maxwell Studio Theatre as well as two outdoor venues, the BMO Stage and the Spiegeltent.

Inspired by the success of the Shaw and Stratford festivals, small towns across Ontario began to convert unused town halls and old opera houses into live theatre venues. In St. Catharines, the FirstOntario Performing Arts Centre and the Essential Collective Theatre both provide performing arts.

The Roselawn Theatre, in the historic lakeside town of Port Colborne, is a part of the Roselawn Centre for the Arts. It is named for the stately three-storey Victorian manor on the grounds. The Showboat Festival began in the 1980s as part of an effort to revitalize downtown Port Colborne. In 1994, the festival moved into the Roselawn Centre for the Arts, where the performance was done in an intimate theatre-in-the-round style, becoming the Showboat Festival Theatre.

In 2002, with declining audience numbers, the Showboat Festival went dark. To keep theatre alive in Port Colborne, Showboat partnered with the Lighthouse Festival in nearby Port Dover. Productions alternated between the two venues each summer, operating under the Lighthouse brand. In 2020, the festival began to operate year-round in the Roselawn Theatre.

In Port Dover, the original Lighthouse Festival in 1905 had begun its historic run in the town's town hall.

Over the years that followed, audiences were treated to a wide variety of acts, ranging from Soap Shows and cure-all hucksters to professional traveling productions such as *Uncle Tom's Cabin* and the Marx Brothers. It was also a venue for locally produced musical and theatrical productions, and was another stop on the travelling vaudeville circuit. Then, due to the modern age of television and movie houses, the theatre went dark in 1958.

That is until 1980 when Brantford's Carpet Bag Theatre troupe moved into the town hall building. After a few renovations, the theatre opened their inaugural season with productions like *The Vaudevillians* and *Gypsy*. The company soon took on a new name, becoming the new Lighthouse Festival Theatre. In 2020, the City of Port Colborne and Lighthouse Festival agreed that Lighthouse could expand their season from the summer to stage live theatre year-round. Productions now occur in both port venues.

Some of this history is on display in the backstage bar area of the Roselawn. Replicas of Showboat playbills are mounted on the wall, along with costumes from past productions.

Art Galleries

In addition to its live theatre, Niagara is also noted for its art galleries. The extensive display of art in the Niagara Falls Art Gallery is noted for its collection of works by renowned Canadian artist William Kurelek. In addition to Kurelek's works of art, the gallery also houses an archive of his personal study materials, acquisitions, fabrications, and promotional materials, even some of his apparel.

Altogether, the Gallery's permanent collection currently contains over 300 works of art, from historic to contemporary. Works by Canadian artists include those by Tony Urquhart, Graham Coughtry, Michael Snow, John MacGregor, and Greg Curnoe. The gallery is located at 8058 Oakwood Drive in Niagara Falls.

Since 2001, The Art Gallery of Welland collection has been housed in the Church House at Central United Church at 12 Yonge Street. As a subsidiary of the Niagara Falls Art Gallery, it is a collective of arts organizations whose aim is to provide arts programming to residents of Welland and area.

Located in the historic village of Queenston, RiverBrink Art Museum at 116 Queenston Street features changing exhibitions from the art collection of Samuel E. Weir, Q.C., as well as those on loan from other Canadian and international collections. Open to the public since 1983, RiverBrink is situated in a large country home on the banks of the scenic Niagara River with well-kept gardens and views of the river. Admission is by donation; the art museum is closed from Sunday to Tuesday.

The Northern Expressions Inuit Art Gallery in Jordan Village has focused on First Nations and Inuit art since 2014. The

Port Dover's historic town hall, although outside the Niagara area, has long held the Showboat Festival and, along with Port Colborne's Lighthouse Festival, creates yet another theatrical hub in the region.

gallery offers soapstone carvings, drawings, and prints, as well as other creative works by accomplished Indigenous artists. The gallery lies on the short but popular main street of Jordan Village.

Across the street from Northern Expressions, the Jordan Art Gallery exhibits contemporary works of fine art and fine craft from the Niagara region. The selections are diverse and evolving, and include paintings, sculptures, mixed media/assemblage, textiles, wood, glass and ceramics from artists working in the region today. The gallery opened in 2000. Along with other boutiques, cafes and the Cave Spring cellars' tours and wine tastings, and its new historic museum, Jordan is becoming an artistic enclave within Niagara's scenic wine country.

Niagara-on-the-Lake also offers a variety of galleries. The King Street Gallery, located at 153 King Street, is housed in one of the town's many historic homes. It features contemporary paintings and works created from a variety of mediums that include wood carvings, sculptures, and turned wood creations, along with glassworks, jewelry, and pottery.

The Gate Street Studio of Sandra Iafrate features her works depicting flowers and other scenes of nature. Ron and Barb Zimmerman's pottery creations are found in Lakeside Pottery, in business since 1989. The Niagara Image Gallery features a collection of works of art that includes limited-edition reproductions and collectibles, plus original pieces by Canadian artists Trisha Romance and Tanya Jean Peterson.

The architecturally striking Niagara Image Gallery in Niagara-on-the-Lake is the family home of the artist Trisha Romance.

THE BEST GRAPES MAKE THE FINEST WINE

Niagara's Wine Country Trails

Part of the answer as to why Niagara is such a great area for growing grapes is that it is on the same latitude as Provence and Languedoc-Roussillon in France, the Chianti Classico region in Italy and the Rioja region in Spain. This means that temperatures in Niagara are similar to those in Bordeaux and Burgundy in France. With the moderating effects of Lakes Ontario and Erie, and the sheltering protection provided by the cliffs of the Niagara Escarpment, the area benefits from moderate temperatures during the spring and summer growing seasons while, during the fall, the warmer air from the lakes generally delays damaging early frosts.

In just a few short decades, the wine industry in Ontario has fermented from a laughingstock, with wine names like Baby Duck, to international award-winning Chardonnays, Merlots and Cabernets. And the Niagara area is considered the heart of Ontario's wine industry. But that isn't where it all began.

In fact, Ontario's first vineyard wasn't in Niagara at all; rather, it was on the banks of the Credit River in modern day Mississauga. Around 1811, a vineyard was planted by a Pennsylvania German immigrant named Johann Schiller and covered an area of

Bottles of popular ice wine on display at the historic Peller Estates Winery.

Young grape vines thrive in the regions climate and soil.

Mechanical grape harvesting is a common sight in Niagara-on-the-Lake.

eight hectares (20 acres). His labrusca vines yielded grape varieties such as Concord and Niagara.

A half-century later, in 1866, Pelee Island, a low-lying slab of limestone at the western end of Lake Erie, then just being occupied by the Europeans, saw the next step forward. Its moderate climate proved ideal for the production of grapes. Ontario's first commercial winery opened on the island and was known as Vin Villa, remnants of which are preserved to this day.

But Niagara wasn't far behind. By 1873, the Ontario Grape Growing and Wine Manufacturing Company began producing Niagara's first wines. However, most of Ontario's wineries remained situated in southwestern Ontario, while the Niagara region concentrated on the production of tender fruit, especially peaches.

In 1973, the Inniskillin winery received Ontario's first wine licence granted since the end of Prohibition. Soon after, in 1978, Château des Charmes and Cave Spring Vineyard began production, and a year later, St. Urban Vineyard (now part of Vineyard Estates), planted 20 hectares (50 acres) of Riesling grapes. 1983 saw the production of Ontario's first ice wines.

Vintners Quality Alliance (VQA)

In 1988, Ontario wine producers established geographic regions and quality standards through the Vintners Quality Alliance (VQA). That paid off three years later when Inniskillin's 1989 Icewine won the prestigious Grand Prix d'Honneur at Vinexpo in Bordeaux, France. Niagara's wine culture became even more firmly established in 1996 when Brock University established a Cool Climate Oenology programme.

In 2000, Niagara College established a course in Winery and Viticulture Technician at its Niagara-on-the-Lake campus. This facility, like the wineries of the region, offers tours and tastings.

More familiar to the wine industry than to the public are the geographic sub-regions, which determine which variety of grape performs best with those soil and climate conditions. Known as "sub-appellations," they include the flat sandy soils near the shore of Lake Ontario, the more rolling terrain further inland and what are known as the "benches" which formed at the base of Niagara's cliffs. Here lies the

Canada's first commercial teaching winery is located on the campus of Niagara College in Niagara-on-the-Lake.

VinVilla on Pelee Island was Ontario's earliest commercial winery.

The Ravine Vineyard Estate Winery occupies a historic building which dates back two centuries.

heart of Niagara's wine industry, between the escarpment and Lake Ontario, and stretching from Grimsby to the Niagara River, with a concentration close to Niagara-on-the-Lake.

Today, Niagara's wine industry can count more than 90 wineries which welcome more than a half million wine connoisseurs each year. Of those wineries, a few stand out.

Wayne Gretzky Estates Winery and Distillery

In Niagara's wine country, one very distinctive winery stands out: the Wayne Gretzky

A sign at the Chateau des Charmes Winery welcomes visitors.

This distillery and winery proudly bears the name of hockey's legendary Great One.

Estates Winery and Distillery. Historically, distilleries were affiliated more with grist mills and seldom with wineries. But this enterprise has both.

The Gretzky winery first opened in 2007, and later affiliated with Peller Estates. Today, it has become one of the more iconic sights on Niagara's wine landscape. A 2100-square-metre estate building includes an outdoor ice rink complete with a loonie buried below the ice surface, recalling the Vancouver Winter Olympics during which Wayne Gretzky secretly buried a loonie at the centre of the hockey rink to bring Team Canada good luck. It worked; both women's and men's teams won gold medals that year.

During the summer the rink becomes a water feature. Summer weather also allows an outdoor patio to serve lunches at the wine bar. Hockey fans may wander inside to see loads of "99" memorabilia including sweaters, photos and some of the Great One's many trophies and also enjoy a wine or whisky tasting experience.

Wine and whisky products, bearing a prominent 99 on the label, include a wide

Vineland Estates Winery

Jackson-Triggs Winery

variety of distilled products, including a 99-proof whisky, as well as vodkas. Wines run the full gamut from Cabernet Sauvignons, Roses, Merlots and more.

The winery is situated prominently on the northeast edge of the roundabout on Niagara Stone Road at the intersection of Line 3, just over seven kilometres from Niagara-on-the-Lake.

Palatine Hills Estate Winery

A short distance from Niagara-on-the-Lake, lies the Palatine Hills Estate Winery. It was here during the War of 1812 that the British

Peller Winery

military regrouped and stationed a garrison following the American sacking of the town of Newark, as Niagara-on-the-Lake was then called.

In 1972, as the land was being prepared to plant grape vines, the owners uncovered cannonballs, coins, and other war remnants which they attributed to the British military. Today, many of those artifacts are on display in the winery, where bottles of their unique 1812 series of wine commemorate the area's involvement in the war.

Reif Estate Winery

The heart of the battleground in the War of 1812 lay between Queenston and Niagara-on-the-Lake, and here sits the Reif Estate Winery on land that has been farmed since the 1780s by Loyalists who fled the United States after the American Revolution. The winery is on the Niagara Parkway, about five kilometres south of Niagara-on-the-Lake.

Blooming peach trees in Niagara region.

Ravine Vineyard Estate Winery

The site of the Ravine Vineyard was a rest stop for Laura Secord during her legendary hike to warn the British of a planned American attack. The site was a strategic location long before that. It marked the junction of two Indigenous trails and was the site of a village of the Neutral tribe. Later, it was also the junction of two settlement roads, the Portage Road opened to bypass the falls, and the York Road from Stoney Creek to Queenston.

In 1802, Loyalist refugee David Secord arrived at the location and built saw and grist mills. These operations attracted other pioneer industries, including a general store and blacksmith shop, and become the village of St. David's. The large Georgian Secord House was home to Laura Secord and her husband James Secord before they relocated to Queenston.

The original house was destroyed by the invaders but was rebuilt, disassembled, and relocated several times before coming to rest back on its original site. In 1867, the Lowrey's began growing the grapes. The Ravine Winery now offers tours, tastings and meals, as well as their signature Ravine Sand & Gravel Riesling and Ravine Meritage wines.

Henry of Pelham Family Estate Winery

This estate once sat on land whose history dates back before the War of 1812, to the American War of Independence. In 1784, the Crown deeded the property to Nicholas Smith in gratitude for his service in the legendary Butler's Rangers, who were a thorn in the side of the American forces during that war. Being part Iroquois, Smith served mainly as translator between Butler's commanders and the many Indigenous warriors who fought with the British and whose tactics were key in terrorizing the enemy.

At the junction of the Pelham Road, which linked Burlington with the Niagara

Inniskillin Niagara Estate Winery

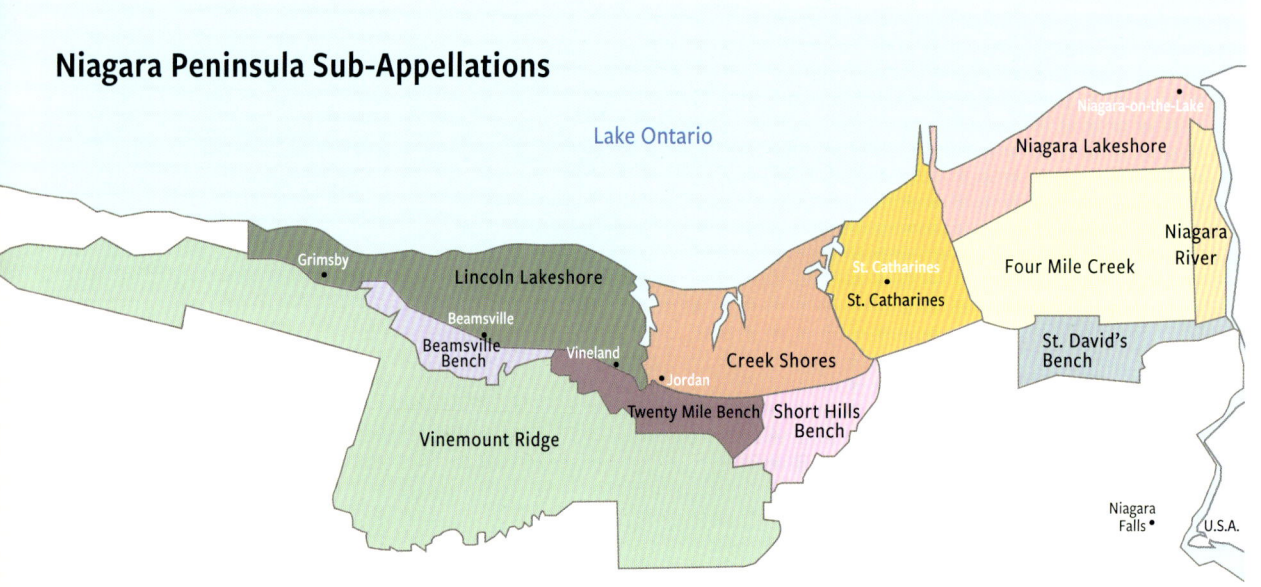

The composition of the soil is very important when growing grapes for fine wine. These regions are officially recognized as distinct grape growing regions by the Vintner's Quality Alliance.

River, and the St. David's Road, Smith's son Henry opened an inn and tavern which he called the Henry of Pelham Inn. Now expanded beyond the original land grant, the property has become the renowned Henry of Pelham Family Estate Winery.

The basement of the current building was the ground floor of the original inn. The original wooden crest of the famed and feared Butler's Rangers sits prominently above the fireplace.

Wine Tours

One way to tour some of the area's wineries and have a drink or two, without the worry of driving, is to join one of the many motor coach wine tours. The Magic Winery Bus, which departs from Niagara-on-the-Lake on a regular schedule, is a 25-seat vehicle. Its website claims that "guests will see firsthand the unique terroir that creates some of the most memorable wines in the world; learn about the region's history and connection with food." The bus departs from the Lakeshore Winery three times on Saturday and Sunday and stops at Trius Winery, the Gretzky Winery as well as the Pillitteri and Pondview wineries.

Niagara Airbus offers a tour that departs from Toronto, tours the Konzelmann Estates, the Pilliteri Estates and the Inniskillin Winery and tops off the day with free time in Niagara-on-the-Lake.

Wine tasting is offered in many of the area's wineries.

Niagara Day Tour covers three wineries and includes a cheese tasting and a visit to a popular chocolate factory followed by free time in Niagara-on-the-Lake.

Mary Morton Tours offers, among a wide variety of tour options such as theatre and lunch cruises, a more comprehensive Niagara package, travelling back roads throughout the region with wine tastings. In all, Mary Morton Tours may take in any of a dozen and a half wineries. Fine quality meals are always part of this long-standing company's many day trip or overnight packages.

For self-drive tours, Niagara's wineries' facilities and locations are all online. Most roads in Niagara's wine country have blue signs, like the one to the right, that indicate the "Wine Route."

NIAGARA-ON-THE-LAKE WINERIES

1. AMO Winery, 976 York Road
2. Bella Terra Vineyards, Line 2 Road
3. Between the Lines Winery, 991 Four Mile Creek Road, RR 4
4. Big Head Wines, 823 Line 6 Road
5. Byland Estate Winery, 834 Line 3 Road
6. Caroline Cellars, 1010 Line 2 Road
7. Château des Charmes, 1025 York Road
8. Colaneri Estate Winery, 348 Concession 6 Road
9. De Simone Vineyards, 865 Niagara Stone Road
10. Drea's Wine Company, 15608 Niagara Parkway, RR 1
11. Ferox by Fabian Reis, 1829 Concession 4 Road
12. Frogpond Farm Organic Winery, 1385 Larkin Road
13. Hare Wine Company, 769 Niagara Stone Road
14. Icellars Estate Winery, 615 Concession 5 Road
15. Inniskillin Niagara Estate Winery 1499, Line 3 at the Niagara Parkway
16. Jackson-Triggs Niagara Estate, 2145 Niagara Stone Road
17. Konzelmann Estate Winery, 1096 Lakeshore Road
18. Lailey Winery, 15940 Niagara River Parkway
19. Lakeview Wine Company, 1067 Niagara Stone Road
20. Marynissen Estates Winery, 1208 Concession 1 Road
21. Niagara College Teaching Winery, 135 Taylor Road
22. NOMAD at Hinterbrook Winery, 1181 Lakeshore Road
23. Palatine Hills Estate Winery, 911 Lakeshore Road
24. Peller Estates Winery and Restaurant, 290 John Street East
25. Pillitteri Estates Winery, 1696 Niagara Stone Road
26. Queenston Mile Vineyard, 963 Queenston Road
27. Ravine Vineyard Estate Winery, 1366 York Road
28. Reif Estate Winery, 15608 Niagara River Parkway RR 1
29. Riverview Cellars Estate Winery, 15376 Niagara Parkway
30. Shiny Apple Cider Home of Fresh Wines, 1242 Irvine Road
31. Southbrook Organic Vineyards, 581 Niagara Stone Road
32. Stratus Vineyards, 2059 Niagara Stone Road
33. Strewn Winery, 1339 Lakeshore Road
34. Trius Winery and Restaurant, 1249 Niagara Stone Road
35. Two Sisters Vineyards, 240 John Street East
36. Wayne Gretzky Estates, 1219 Niagara Stone Road

NIAGARA REGION WINERIES

ST. CATHARINES

13th Street Winery
1776 Fourth Avenue

Henry of Pelham Family Estate Winery
1469 Pelham Road

Hernder Estate Wines
1607 Eighth Avenue Louth

King's Court Estate Winery
2083 Seventh Street, Louth

Rockway Vineyards
3290 Ninth Street

Wending Home Estate Vineyards and Winery
3756 Ninth Street

JORDAN

16 Mile Cellar
3555 Eleventh Street

180 Estate Winery
4055 Nineteenth Street

Calamus Estate Winery
3100 Glen Road

Cave Spring Vineyard
3836 Main Street

Creekside Estate Winery
2170 Fourth Avenue

Flat Rock Cellars
2727 Seventh Avenue

Harbour Estates Winery
4362 Jordan Road

Honsberger Estate Winery
4060 Jordan Road

Sue-Ann Staff Estate Winery
3210 Staff Avenue

Westcott Vineyards
3180 Seventeenth Street

VINELAND

Alvento Winery
3048 Second Avenue

Cloudsley Cellars
3795 Victoria Avenue

Featherstone Estate Winery
3678 Victoria Avenue

Foreign Affair Winery
4890 Victoria Avenue North

Greenlane Estate Winery
3751 King Street

Kacaba Vineyards & Winery
3550 King Street

London Born Wine Company
4000 Cherry Avenue

Megalomaniac Wines
3930 Cherry Avenue

Niagara Custom Crush Studio
3201 King Street

Rennie Estate Winery
3201 King Street

Ridgepoint Wines
3900 Cherry Avenue

Royal DeMaria Wines
4551 Cherry Avenue

Stoney Ridge Estate Winery
3201 King Street

Tawse Winery
3955 Cherry Avenue

Vineland Estates Winery
3620 Moyer Road

BEAMSVILLE

Back 10 Cellars
4101 King Street

Cave Spring Vineyard
4043 Cave Spring Road

Commisso Estate Winery
564 Kemp Road East

Cornerstone Estate Winery
4390 Tufford Road

Good Earth Food and Wine Co.
4556 Lincoln Avenue

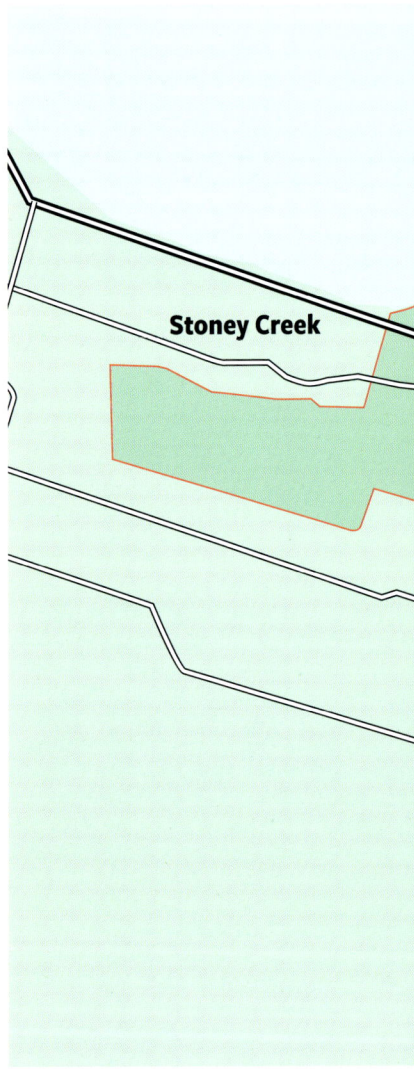

Hidden Bench Estate Winery
4152 Locust Lane

Legends Estates Winery
4888 Ontario Street North

Locust Lane Estate Winery
4041 Locust Lane

Magnotta Winery
4701 Ontario Street

Malivoire Wine Company
4260 King Street East

Organized Crime Winery
4043 Mountainview Road

Peninsula Ridge Estates Winery
5600 King Street West

Redstone Winery and Restaurant
4245 King Street

Rosewood Winery & Meadery
4352 Mountainview Road

Thirty Bench Wine Makers
4281 Mountainview Road

Vieni Estates Wine & Spirits
4553 Fly Road

Villa Romana Estate Winery
4746 King Street

STONEY CREEK

Leaning Post Wines
1491 Highway 8

Puddicombe Estate Winery
1468 Highway 8

Ridge Road Estate Winery
1205 Ridge Road

LINCOLN

Black Bank Hill
4247 Sann Road

SAINT ANNS

Domaine Queylus
3651 Sixteen Road

DAY TRIPS AND EXPLORATIONS — HISTORY

FLAMES ACROSS THE BORDER

The Legacy of the War of 1812

Friendly neighbours now, the United States and Canada boast that theirs is the longest undefended international border in the world. But that wasn't always the case.

On June 18, 1812, President James Madison declared war on Britain and set out to capture the lands north of the Great Lakes, thinking it would be an easy victory. The United States Secretary of War boldly stated that "We can take Canada without soldiers, we have only to send officers into the province, and the people will rally around our standards." Time would prove that to be overly optimistic, indeed a fatal miscalculation.

With the two nations separated by wide and windy lakes, the most logical places to cross the border to invade Canada were at the Detroit and Niagara rivers. As the latter was closer to the American population centres and military routes, the area around Niagara became the main battleground and today has many monuments and historical sites that commemorate those battles.

Fort George, the scene of pivotal battles during the War of 1812, is now rebuilt as a National Historic Site.

Previous spread: **Monument at Queenston Heights to War of 1812 heroine Laura Secord.**

On September 30, 1811, Britain assigned Major-General Isaac Brock to Upper Canada as administrator of the colony and commander of the armed forces. His job was to defend against looming American attacks and, strategically, to enlist the aid of Tecumseh and his feared warriors to the British side.

On October 13, 1812, there occurred the most famous battle of the war, the Battle of Queenston Heights. As American forces struggled to make their way across the Niagara River beneath the massive limestone gateway which formed the entrance to the Niagara Gorge, General Brock, alerted by the distant rumble of cannonfire, burst forth from Fort George in Newark (Niagara-on-the-Lake) and galloped to the battle on his horse, Alfred. However, no sooner had he arrived and rallied his troops than a sniper's bullet pierced his chest, killing him. Chief John Norton, an adopted Mohawk and warrior chief, held the Americans off until reinforcements arrived led by General Sir Roger Hale Sheaffe. The British forces and First Nations fighters sent the invaders scurrying back across the river in confusion. In the process the British captured 1,000 Americans.

Battles raged across the front in the Maritimes, along the St. Lawrence, and in American territory as well. Things began to turn in Britain's favour when, on June 6, British troops launched a surprise nighttime attack on an American encampment at Stoney Creek, forcing the Americans to flee back across the peninsula to the river and abandon their siege of Fort Erie.

Laura Secord

Meanwhile, back at Queenston, a young woman named Laura Secord overheard American officers, billeted at her house, discussing a plan of attack at a location known as Beaver Dams. She slipped out unnoticed in the dark and made her way to the headquarters of Lieutenant James FitzGibbon, high atop the Escarpment, to warn him of the plans. Thus alerted, FitzGibbon sent 400 Indigenous warriors to the site of Beaver Dams, along with a few British regulars, culminating in the most decisive Indigenous victory of the war—celebrated as the Battle of Beaver Dams.

The Laura Secord Homestead is a popular attraction.

Meanwhile, the Canadian militia had captured Fort Schlosser on the American side of the Niagara River. Then, on July 8, 1813, at Butler's Farm, at the very southern end of Butler Street in Niagara-on-the-Lake, a force of Norton's warriors surprised an American encampment near Fort George, killing or capturing all.

Then, during a bitter winter blizzard on December 10, 1813, the Americans fled Fort George, burning the town of Newark as they did. A little more than a week later, the British, along with their First Nations allies, captured Fort Niagara on the opposite shore of the river without a shot being fired. They then went on to destroy the nearby village of Lewiston in retaliation for the burning of Newark.

But the British weren't done yet, as they then marched on to burn the villages of Black Rock and Buffalo.

The Americans, however, weren't done either. In July, they recaptured Fort Erie and defeated a sizeable British force at Chippawa a short distance downstream. After these victories, the Americans marched on the small village of St. David's at the base of the escarpment, not far from Queenston and put it to the torch.

Then, on July 25, 1814, Lundy's Lane witnessed the bloodiest battle of the war. Chief

John Norton, along with a sizeable force of troops and Indigenous warriors, defeated the Americans, with staggering losses of 900 men on each side.

Finally, in August of 1814, representatives of both sides met in Belgium to sign the Treaty of Ghent, meant to end hostilities. But it took until Christmas Eve before the treaty was finally ratified.

Brock's Monument

Because of the significance of Niagara in the war, monuments, plaques, and historic structures abound throughout the region.

The most prominent of them is the lofty monument to General Isaac Brock situated in Queenston Heights Park. His heroic charge at the pivotal battle of Queenston Heights turned him into the hero of the war, even though he was killed early in that battle. The first monument to Brock was erected in 1823, but was bombed by a terrorist in 1840. Designed by William Thomas, the current monument was completed in 1853. Rising 56 metres into the air, the monument is one of the world's tallest. Visitors may enter through a gallery and climb to a viewing platform at the top.

Atop the column, four outward-facing figures depict victory, while rising above them is the statue to the hero himself, measuring 4.8 metres in height. At the base of the monument, as described by Parks Canada: "...military trophies of classical

The iconic monument to General Sir Isaac Brock, the hero of the Battle of Queenston Heights, dominates the escarpment high above Queenston.

Fort Erie was reconstructed to offer visitors a look at military life in the 19th century.

armour stand at the corners of a low, enclosing wall set on a slightly elevated platform; the many sculpted elements including the military trophies, the rampant lions, the bas reliefs, the elaborate capital on the column, and the other flutings and mouldings that grace the monument. The circular staircase of 235 stone blocks is lighted by openings placed at intervals that lead to the viewing deck at the top of the monument. The crypt under the floor contains the tombs of General Brock and Colonel Macdonell."

A commemorative plaque, among the several on the grounds, honours the man who came to the rescue of the Canadians, General Sir Roger Hale Sheaffe.

Landscape of Nations Memorial

While Brock is considered the hero of the day, were it not for the Indigenous warriors and their war cries, which intimidated the Americans, the battle would have been lost. These warriors held off the attackers until General Sheaffe arrived with reinforcements from Fort George. And so, it is fitting that a special memorial should honour their bravery on the battlefield. Situated in the shadow of the Brock Monument, is the Landscape of Nations memorial, a tribute to the various Indigenous warriors who valiantly aided the British in their defense of Canada. The display depicts the turtle,

Fort Mississauga, a National Historic Site which now sits in a golf course, is a ghost fort from the War of 1812.

which represents the Earth, and a statue of John Norton, the Mohawk leader who commanded the Indigenous forces, not just at Queenston Heights but also at the pivotal battles of Stoney Creek and Chippawa.

Sharing the display is a statue of Chief John Brant, son of Joseph Brant (who had led the Mohawks to the banks of the Grand River years earlier. Besides his military achievements, Brant was also a strong advocate for local schools. He went on to become the resident superintendent of the Six Nations of the Grand River and was elected an MPP for the riding of Haldimand.

Leading into the centre of the feature, a row of steel arches represents the traditional longhouse, the place of nations living together in peace. The winding walkway represents the Two-Row Wampum Belt, the first treaty between the First Nations and the Europeans. At the centre of the feature, eight limestone walls radiate from the circle while inside the circle is a garden of sweetgrass, a sacred medicine among Indigenous nations across North America.

The beautiful Queenston Heights Restaurant, built in 1939, offers lunch and dinner, and dramatic views of the river and its banks far below and Lake Ontario.

At the stunning viewpoint on the Niagara Parkway, partway up the hill between Queenston and the Brock Monument in Queenston Heights Park, a sign points down a set of steps to the redan. Like a gun battery, a redan is a gun emplacement. And this one played a key role in holding the Americans at bay as they struggled up the escarpment to the heights. Excavated only in 1975, and almost hidden in the forest, the gun itself still sits where it was the day it was last fired.

Fort Drummond

As kids splash around in the wading pool at Queenston Heights Park, they would be unlikely to realize that they are inside what is left of Fort Drummond. This small fortification was built in 1814 to guard the vital portage route from Chippawa to Queenston. Safely inland to avoid cannonfire from the opposite shore, the fort consisted of a U-shaped battery along with a blockhouse that could house 100 troops. After the war, it fell into disuse. Today, it forms the foundation for the wading pool in the southern portion of Queenston Heights Park.

Besides the soaring Brock Monument, Niagara offers important historic buildings and sites, and numerous cairns and historic plaques that reflect the story of this conflict. Three forts, now restored, played a key role in the defence of the region.

Fort Mississauga

Guarding the mouth of the Niagara River is Fort Mississauga. Built in 1814 to supplement Fort George, it is a rare style of fortification, with a simple tower, surrounded by surviving earthworks. The original complex included barracks, a guardroom, and cells to house the prisoners of war. Although the troops had vacated the fort by 1826, they moved back in 1837 due to the threat posed by the Upper Canada Rebellion, and again in 1854 due to disputes with American expansionists. It was staffed once more during the American Civil War and finally with the threat posed by the Fenian Brotherhood. By 1870, it had served its purpose and has sat as a ruin ever since.

In the early decades of the 19th century, it served as a lighthouse. When the 1804 lighthouse at Mississauga Point, the first lighthouse in Canada, was dismantled in 1814, the light was reinstalled on Fort Mississauga. New range lights at the mouth of the Niagara River were put into operation on October 10, 1904. In 1937, the Canadian government placed a plaque on the wall of the fort to commemorate the lighthouse.

The Historic Sites and Monuments Board of Canada designated Fort Mississauga a National Historic Site in 1960. Since that time, efforts have been made to stabilize the structure. It sits in Niagara-on-the-Lake, overlooking the Niagara River; the American Fort Niagara is visible on the far side of the river. Surrounded by a golf course, the grounds contain historic plaques describing the role and construction of the fort. The stabilized ruins are a ghostly reminder of the role this fortification played during that war.

Fort George

This strategic fortification was built between 1796 and 1799 and was instrumental in the defense of Niagara during the War of 1812. In 1921, the federal government declared the fort and battlefield a

National Historic Site. In 1937, as part of a Depression-era works projects, the government undertook to reconstruct it. Unfortunately, so complete was the devastation from the war that only one original building, the stone powder magazine, had survived.

Today, the reconstructed fort serves as one of Niagara's most visited historic attractions. Guides tour visitors around the site, recounting life within the fort. Guards in authentic tunics participate in musketry displays, while the sounds of a fife and drum corps echo within the ramparts. It is located on Queen's Parade in Niagara-on-the-Lake. The historic plaque to commemorate the battle of Fort George lies close by, at the north end of Queen Street.

Butler's Barracks

Close at hand is the Butler's Barracks National Historic Site. Located in the Paradise Grove woodlands, it was named after Colonel John Butler who commanded a Loyalist military unit during the American Revolutionary War.

In 1871, it became a training ground for the Canadian Expeditionary Force and for Canadian Forces in World War I. It continued to be used for training troops during World War II as well as the Korean War. Butler's Barracks continued to serve the military until the 1960s. The interior of the men's barracks has been refurbished to function as a meeting space for a Parks Canada field unit office. Work was also completed on the commissariat stores and quarters. While visitors may not enter the structure, they may stroll the grounds of Paradise Grove and view the murals and historic plaques.

Fort Erie

The third of the Niagara restored fortifications is Old Fort Erie. Built in 1764, the first fort was originally situated closer to the river, serving as a supply depot for British troops during the American Revolutionary War. Storm damage in 1803 meant a new fort was needed. It was built further inland and constructed of stone.

Even though the fort was by then in ruins, the Fenian invaders of 1866 used it as a base to advance their attacks on Canada. Following that failed invasion, local visitors began to use the ruins and the grounds as a pleasant location for picnics.

In the 1930s, the federal and provincial governments undertook to restore the fort, which is now managed by the Niagara Parks Commission. It is also a National Historic Site where costumed interpreters show visitors the lifestyles of the era, as well as military drills.

DeCew House

Built by John Decou (an alternative spelling) in 1808, the two-storey stone house became the military headquarters of Lieutenant James FitzGibbon in 1813. Decou and his family had fled to Burlington Heights as the war closed in on them.

In June of 1813, a sweating and dishevelled young woman appeared at FitzGibbon's door. Her name was Laura Secord, and she had just trekked from her home in Queenston where she had overheard some billeted American officers discussing a plan of attack at the Beaver Dams Creek. Thus alerted, on June 24, FitzGibbon surprised and easily defeated the Americans at the Battle of Beaver Dams.

Many of those who fought and died in the bloody Battle of Lundy's Lane lie in the Drummond Hill cemetery.

After the war, the Decous moved back to the house and remained there until 1942, when the Hydro-Electric Power Commission of Ontario purchased the property to allow for a reservoir for a power dam. In 1950, a fire destroyed the building, leaving only the stone foundations.

In 2011, recognizing the historical significance of the site, the City of Thorold purchased the property and stabilized the stone foundations, and the site became another National Historic Site of Canada. Plaques describe the historic significance of the house and the Battle of Beaver Dams. Beside the foundation, a First Nations learning circle acknowledges the First Nations ownership of the land and their contribution to the British success in the War of 1812.

McFarland House

Built in 1800, making it one of Niagara's oldest dwellings, this large Georgian house was used during the War of 1812 as a hospital, by both sides in turn, and as a British battery. When McFarland returned following the war, the house was in ruins, but he repaired the structure and it remained in the family for many generations. Today, it serves as a period museum operated by the Niagara Parks Commission. McFarland House lies on the Niagara Parkway, near the southern outskirts of Niagara-on-the-Lake.

Indigenous Warriors Monument

On Queenston Street in the village of Queenston, a monument pays tribute to the First Nations warriors who bravely aided the British military throughout the war. The plaque describes the efforts of Chief

John Norton, who was part Cherokee and part Scot, to bring together the Six Nations of the Grand River to join the British effort to repulse the attempted American invasion. The plaque was erected by the Niagara Parks Commission and the Queenston Community Association.

Brock's Cenotaph

In the shadow of the cliff upon which the Battle of Queenston Heights raged sits Brock's Cenotaph, near the very spot where he was killed. The cenotaph was dedicated by the Prince of Wales on September 18, 1860.

Within the same parkette, visitors will find the bronze monument to Alfred, Brock's beloved horse. Here, Brock had tethered Alfred while he led a charge on foot which led to his death. Colonel Macdonell leapt onto Alfred's saddle to lead another charge against the Americans while General Sheaffe arrived from Fort George to turn back the invaders. Macdonell was also killed. Some allege that Alfred met the same fate, although others contend that he lived out his remaining years in Goderich. Two plaques within Queenston Heights Park commemorate General Sheaffe. One is mounted in the Queenston Heights Restaurant, and the other is on the Brock Monument itself. Three plaques describe the battle.

Battle of Lundy's Lane

In July of 1814, bitter fighting near the village of Drummondville is considered the bloodiest battle ever fought on Canadian soil. When the six-hour battle finally ended with no clear winner, the British casualties included 84 dead and 559 wounded, while the American losses were 174 killed and 572 wounded.

The battlefield was designated a National Historic Site of Canada in 1937. Today, arching across Lundy's Lane is a memorial arch, erected in July of 2014 to mark the 200th anniversary of the bloody fight. The arch portrays a silhouette of troops and weapons and was designed by Jeff Claydon.

In the adjacent church parking lot is the site of the funeral pyre on which the bodies of the fallen soldiers were cremated, since there was insufficient room to bury them. A battle memorial was created by the Canadian Parliament and unveiled by the Lundy's Lane Historical Society on July 25, 1895. The large cairn marks the remains of 22 British soldiers who were buried in the vault below it. Separate plaques honour Laura Secord who is also buried there, and a number of British commanders. There is also a monument to the Unknown American Soldier. Four commemorative panels were erected on the retaining wall at the Drummond Hill Cemetery, facing Lundy's Lane.

Situated across Lundy's Lane from the cemetery, the Battle Ground Hotel Museum is in a restored 1850s tavern which focusses on the history of the battle and offers tours of the sites.

The newly renovated Niagara Falls History Museum is situated just east of the battlefield. It offers visitors a chance to view uniforms and artifacts of that military era. Among the displays, the Gale Family

The Lundy's Lane battlefield memorial arch.

War of 1812 Gallery includes uniforms, weaponry, and equipment relating to the Battle of Lundy's Lane. The museum also commemorates the contributions of the Indigenous warriors who aided the British.

This history museum should not be confused with the Niagara Military Museum, which honours the military history of Niagara and Canadians during World War I, World War II and the Korean War. Displays include military artifacts including uniforms, firearms and photographs. This museum is fittingly located in the historic Niagara Falls Armoury at 5049 Victoria Avenue in the city of Niagara Falls.

Battle of Cook's Mills Cairn

A plaque which commemorates the Battle of Cook's Mills sits in a stone cairn at the intersection of Lyons Creek and Matthews Roads. This battle raged in October of 1814, when the Americans advanced from Fort Erie to the British line at Chippawa Creek. Despite being victorious in the skirmish, the American forces joined the overall retreat the following day.

Battle of Frenchman's Creek

Between Chippawa and Fort Erie, Frenchman's Creek flows into the Niagara River. In November of 1812, the Americans tried

A musket demonstration for visitors to Fort George.

to recover from their losses at Queenston Heights by capturing a British battery at this location. Despite some initial success, they were soon repulsed by British reinforcements and retreated to the American shore.

Battle of Chippawa

The stone cairn by the bridge over the Welland River in Chippawa, on the southern outskirts of Niagara Falls, describes one of the last battles fought during the war (the legendary Battle of New Orleans occurred after the war had formally ended). The words describe the defeat of the Americans, and the end of their efforts to claim Canada as American territory.

Battle of Ridgeway

The War of 1812 was not the only occasion which saw a military incursion from the United States into Canada. Based in the United States, the Fenian Brotherhood were Irish nationalist zealots who tried to free Ireland from British rule, in part by taking British North America hostage. In 1866, one of their incursions was across the Niagara River and into Fort Erie, where they fought and won the Battle of Ridgeway further inland, but the Americans themselves, also anxious to put down the Fenians, cut off their reinforcements. Finally, the threat of an advancing force of Canadian troops reinforced by British regulars led to the Fenian retreat across the border.

Ridgeway Battlefield National Historic Site of Canada is located on four hectares of land south of Ridgeway and five kilometres west of the town of Fort Erie. The site contains a large commemorative stone cairn.

Other War of 1812 Plaques and Cairns

Several historic plaques dedicated to the deadly war lie along the Niagara Parkway. A short distance south of Niagara-on-the-Lake, one such plaque describes the British capture of Fort Niagara on the opposite shore of the river, in December 1813. This one sits by the Parkway opposite East-West Line. Nearby stands a plaque recounting the site of Vrooman's Battery gun emplacement beside the Parkway.

In the community of St. David's, a plaque at the corner of Four Mile Creek Road and St. David's Road (now Regional Road 81) recounts the burning of the town in July of 1814. Following the devastation, the American officer responsible, Colonel Isaac Stone, was censured and relieved of his rank for having destroyed private property.

Some of the pivotal battles of the war occurred west of Niagara. The surprise nighttime raid on an American encampment at Stoney Creek in 1813 sent the advancing Americans fleeing in disarray. But their retreat encountered further fire when at Forty Mile Creek, a British flotilla offshore bombarded the beleaguered troops. A stone cairn in Grimsby recounts this debacle.

A solitary cannon, known as a "redan," sits in its original location below the Queenston lookout on the Niagara Parkway.

GETTING AROUND
Niagara's Historic Highways

The region's first roads were the forest trails used by Indigenous peoples. Portage Road today still follows much of the original First Nations bypass around the falls. Mountain and Beaverdams Roads likewise generally follow those original footpaths, as does today's busy Lundy's Lane.

Following the American Revolution, Loyalist settlers fleeing the persecutions of post-revolutionary America settled in the Niagara Peninsula. At first, they followed existing Indigenous trails, but as settlement proceeded into more of the First Nations land, these trails were improved, straightened, or extended to accommodate the carts and wagons of the settlers.

Surveyors spread across Niagara to lay out a network of concession and side roads to facilitate access to the farm lots. Taverns and rest stops appeared along the new roads, and villages and hamlets sprang up at key intersections. In short order, these surveyed roads came to dominate the landscape, their straight lines often ignoring the topographic obstacles of the terrain.

An aerial view of River Road as it passes Queen Victoria Park on the left and the historic travellers' rest shelter on the right.

The tiny Living Water Wayside Chapel attracts visitors along the Niagara Parkway near Niagara-on-the-Lake.

THE NIAGARA PARKWAY

"The prettiest Sunday afternoon drive in the world." Those were not words from a Niagara tourist brochure, but rather from a crusty world leader named Winston Churchill.

It didn't start that way, however. For many centuries, what became the Niagara Parkway was little more than an Indigenous trail along the bank of the Niagara River. In 1785, British surveyor Augustus Jones set aside a military reserve along the trail and by 1791, it had become the main military route linking Fort Mississauga and Fort Erie. During the War of 1812, it was a key link in Britain's defence network. A chain reserve of 66 feet (one chain) was surveyed along the river to allow the government a strategic military route in case of emergency. The chain reserve still exists on the Niagara Parkway.

After the Niagara Parks Commission began work on the river route in 1908. The 55-kilometre roadway was eventually completed in 1931. Its scenic attributes quickly became apparent. In 1943, British Prime Minister Winston Churchill had taken a break from a secret Quebec City conference with President Roosevelt and Prime Minister Mackenzie King, to visit Niagara

Falls. It was during this visit that he uttered the oft-repeated claim that the Niagara Parkway was the "prettiest Sunday afternoon drive in the world." Thanks to land use restrictions and careful maintenance, the route can still cling to that claim. The Parkway today is lined with scenic lookouts and historic sites and markers. It also offers an unparalleled insight into the geology and history of the region.

From the refurbished National Historic Site of Fort George to Queenston, the road offers views of the river where many pullouts and viewpoints give drivers opportunities to stretch or take photos. After passing vineyards, the Parkway comes to one of the route's more historic locations, the McFarland House.

At Line 1 Road, about four kilometres from the fort, the Parkway passes what is considered Ontario's smallest church, the Living Water Wayside Chapel. Built in 1964 by the Christian Reformed Church, this eight-square-metre place of worship can fit about six people comfortably in the four pews. They may also be interested in the Walker's Country Market next door, which has been a landmark on the Parkway since the 1930s.

From the Parkway, Line 3 leads a short distance west to the Croatian National Centre and the Inniskillin wineries, one of the region's first. At Brown's Point is a parking lot and plaque for the site of a British battery during the War of 1812.

The Rotary Clock on the River Road section of the Niagara Parkway, opposite the American Falls, marks the 100th anniversary of the Rotary Club of Niagara Falls.

A rare fence soon comes into view on the river side of the road. Known as an Irish dry-stone wall, it consists of rock slabs which are piled atop each other to create a fence with no mortar between the stones. Behind that fence lies one of Niagara's grander homes, Glencairn.

Between this fence line and Queenston, the view of the river from the Parkway has been obscured by large private homes. Queenston Street veers left from the Parkway to lead into historic Queenston with such attractions as the Laura Secord Homestead, the Mackenzie Printery, the historic Willowbank Manor atop a high hill, and the memorial cairns to General Brock and his horse, Alfred.

From Queenston, the Parkway winds steeply up the face of the Escarpment. From a viewpoint at the crest of the cliff, a stunning view extends down the river. A staircase leads from the parking area to a War of 1812 gun emplacement known as the Queenston Heights Redan.

Then the Parkway follows the rim of the Niagara Gorge to Queenston Heights Park, with its trails and its historic monuments. These include the soaring Brock's Monument and one to Laura Secord. The park includes the Bruce Trail Terminis Cairn, as well as the new Indigenous Landscape of Nations Memorial. The historic Queenston Heights Restaurant provides meals with a view.

The Parkway continues past a roundabout, beside which a trail leads to the Lotus Grove parking lot. A peaceful island of tranquility away from the traffic of the Parkway, the area features a grove of majestic lotus trees and views into the gorge. The sign to it is rather small, however, so look carefully.

Floral Clock

The roadway then passes beneath Highway 402 and the Queenston Lewiston Bridge to come face to face with the iconic Floral Clock. Other than the falls, it is one of Niagara's most photographed sites. Measuring 12 metres in diameter, the face of the clock contains up to 16,000 plants. It was designed and planted by horticulturalists and students from the Niagara Parks School of Horticulture. Based on a 1903 clock in the Princes Street Gardens of Edinburgh, Scotland, the Niagara clock is the largest of its kind in the world, three times the size of that in Scotland. The clock was completed in 1950 and is maintained by Ontario Hydro. Behind the clock, a tower rings the Westminster chimes every quarter hour.

The route then takes a sudden industrial turn passing atop the massive Sir Adam Beck Generating Stations which supplies much of the power to Ontario's electrical grid.

A short distance further along are the entrances to the Butterfly Conservatory and Botanical Gardens which are covered in their own chapters elsewhere in this book.

The Niagara Glen, known for its unusual rock formations and its Carolinian forest, provides challenging hiking opportunities for ardent hikers and even rock climbers. The Nature Centre there offers a trove of

After Niagara Falls itself, the historic Floral Clock on the Niagara Parkway near the Sir Adam Beck Power Plant, is one of the most photographed attractions in the region.

information on the geology, flora, and fauna in the Glen.

For those keen on more hiking to the river, just beyond WildPlay Niagara at Whirlpool Park, a steep trail leads right down to the whirlpool itself. The cliffs that tower over the trail are in fact the walls of the pre-glacial gully known as the St. David's Buried Gorge, through which the river flowed eons ago before the melting glaciers plugged it up with debris. This obstacle forced the river to make its abrupt 90-degree turn which created the bay in which the river swirls to form the famous whirlpool. This two-kilometre trail is steep and uneven and includes steps, but once at the bottom, the whirlpool is right there. If the hike is too challenging, there

A late summer day along the beautiful Niagara Parkway shows why the area is so popular with visitors.

is a viewpoint atop the cliff opposite the entrance to the WildPlay park.

At Victoria Avenue, which forks off to the right, the Parkway becomes River Road and enters a more urban landscape. River Road leads past the crowds in the area around Clifton Hill and past the beauty of the falls and Queen Victoria Park. Then, from the Old Scow Lookout and Dufferin Islands further along, it again resumes is route as the Niagara Parkway.

Chippawa and Navy Island

Continuing along the Niagara Parkway past Dufferin Islands, you come to Chippawa. A historic plaque describes the pivotal Battle of Chippawa in the 1812 conflict while across the river lies Navy Island. Navy Island became the centre of a national controversy during the Rebellion of 1837, when William Lyon Mackenzie, leader of the rebels, and 700 of his "patriots" occupied the island. It was here that one of the more famous incidents of the rebellion took place—the burning of the steamer *Caroline*. This supply ship, which had been rented by Mackenzie, was captured by the British forces on December 29, 1837. It was set ablaze and sent over the falls.

Beyond the marker, the Willoughby Historical Museum, established in 1968 in a former schoolhouse, contains a trove of genealogical information as well as regional artifacts and documents.

The Parkway here hugs the low riverbank and the river itself, free of its tormented rapids, is wide and more tranquil. At Black Creek Road, the Lighthouse Restaurant, housed in a former lighthouse that dates to the early 1800s, is a popular Parkway dining spot.

The road crosses Black Creek on an early stone bridge before heading to the Switch Road, a sideroad which leads to the Elope Niagara Little Log Wedding Chapel. Set amid a wooded grove at the end of a private road, this tiny chapel is not a public tourist attraction; rather, it is there for private weddings.

Before entering Fort Erie, the Parkway comes to the Frenchman's Creek National Historic Site, where a fading plaque embedded in a stone cairn outlines a failed attempt by American forces during the War of 1812 to sever communications between British forces at Fort Erie and Chippawa.

The Parkway maintains its riverbank location before passing under the International Railway Bridge, a historic structure dating from 1873, and into the core of Fort Erie itself. Beyond Bertie Street the Parkway is no longer the Parkway, but an urban street named Niagara Boulevard. At Bertie Street a plaque and park mark the location of the historic ferry landing which served the town from 1796 to 1950.

After passing beneath the Peace Bridge, the Niagara Parkway ends at the Mather Park and Arch, a monument dedicated to William Mather, the major proponent of the Peace Bridge.

Jarvis Street marks the main street of Fort Erie, a community which evolved from its early role as a landing spot. When the railway bridge opened and the railways established stations and yards in the town, ferry service was discontinued.

Portage Road

This bypass around the falls followed an earlier Indigenous portage between Chippawa at the mouth of the Welland River, and Queenston, the head of navigation from Lake Ontario on the Niagara River. This became the first coach route in Upper Canada, as Ontario was called at the time. Three times a week, a traveller could ride for $1.00 each way. Opened in 1789 by a group of private traders led by Robert Hamilton, the road became an official government highway in 1791.

The highway remained one of Upper Canada's first transportation links between the two Great Lakes until the opening of the Welland Canal in 1829. Businesses appeared along the Portage Road, as did the accommodations for early visitors to the falls. Where the Portage Road intersected with Lundy's Lane, another of the region's key early routes, the settlement of Drummondville grew up. W.H. Smith in 1853 described Drummondville as "an agreeable place of residence were it not for the continuous monotonous rumbling sound of the [Falls]."

The first tourists converged on the intersection coming by horseback, stagecoach, wagon, or even on foot. Smith goes on to describe Lundy's Lane as having "two observatories for the accommodation of visitors, the highest of which is said to be 80 feet in height." Tourists needed accommodation and the inns along the Portage Road filled those needs. As tourism grew with the arrival of the railways, Portage Road evolved into an urban corridor lined with homes, businesses and places of amusement.

Portage Road today, although much widened and straightened, largely follows much of its original alignment. From the bridge in Chippawa today it mounts the bluff overlooking the Dufferin Islands. It then branches to the right from Marineland Parkway, passing Harry Oakes' grand old mansion, Oak Hall.

When the road reaches the entrance to the Incline Railway, it heads left and passes between the Embassy Suites and the Oakes Hotel. After passing the intersection with Stanley Avenue, it changes names and becomes Main Street. The cluster of businesses at its intersection with Lundy's Lane represent the present site of the pioneer village of Drummondville. The Niagara Falls History Museum, and the Battle of Lundy's Lane historic site in the Drummond Hill Cemetery, are both within a short distance of the intersection.

Main Street continues north and today passes through a primarily residential area, resuming the name Portage Road past North Street. When it reaches Morrison Street, it is forced to divert to the west due to the Hydro Canal, which leads to the Sir Adam Beck Power Station. It picks up again past the canal and continues to Neil Street where it becomes a narrower roadway and angles to the right, finally coming to an end at the hydro reservoir.

Despite the urban sprawl which dominates the route, a number of historic locations provide a look into the road's past history. Among them is the Halfway Carriage House, now a popular B&B, at 2495 Stanley Avenue, about nine kilometres from Oak Hall.

The Whirlpool House at 3011 Portage Road dates from 1796, making it one of the oldest surviving structures on the Portage Road. Built by Andrew Rorback, it was at first a saddlery prior to serving the travelling public as Rorback's Tavern. It is situated at the corner of Portage Road and Church's Lane.

At 3428 Portage Road, where Portage Road converges with Stanley Avenue, St. John's Anglican Church dates from 1825 and is one of Ontario's oldest Anglican churches. Restored in 1985, it features gothic windows and buttresses along its southern wall.

At the intersection of Portage Road and Norton Street, on the northern fringes of Chippawa, stands Holy Trinity Church. It dates from 1840 following the burning of its 1820 predecessor by Mackenzie's rebels. Sitting back from the road, it displays an English Gothic revival style of architecture and has a stunning steeple. The 1820 date on the front of the building refers to the 1820 origin of the earlier building. Among those who worshipped here were King Edward VII, Laura Secord, and Jenny Lind.

An early home, and former tavern, still stands on the Portage Road north of Niagara Falls.

Located at 4891 Portage Road, the John Thompson house is another one of the oldest buildings along this thoroughfare. This stone house, constructed in 1825 by its owner John Thomson Jr., is a striking example of Loyalist architecture with a gable roof and symmetrical front façade.

Number 5091 Portage Road is a storey-and-a-half home with a pair of dormers above the pillared porch. Known as the Compton House, it dates from 1840.

Queen Elizabeth Way

By the 1930s, intercity traffic volumes between Toronto and Hamilton had begun to overwhelm Highway 2 and the route needed improvement. A new road was contemplated as a limited access freeway, the first in North America. It became officially known as the Queen Elizabeth Way (QEW) to commemorate the first Royal visit to Canada by King George VI and Queen Elizabeth (the Queen Mother) in 1939.

Queen Elizabeth was delighted with the honour and agreed to attend a special dedication ceremony near the Henley Bridge in St. Catharines on June 7, 1939. To commemorate the royal opening, monuments were placed at the highway's original beginning and end points. That at Toronto's Humber River bridge was the Lion Monument, designed by William Lyon Somerville and sculpted by Frances Loring. It displays a snarling British lion atop a high column and was partly inspired by British resolve at the start of World War II. He also designed the monuments at the two ends of the Henley Bridge in St. Catharines. The monument in Toronto was moved to Sunnyside Park beside the Humber River to make way for

The Lion Monument marks the Toronto terminus of the original route of the Queen Elizabeth Way. A smaller monument remains on the highway in St. Catharines.

reconstruction of the highway. In St. Catharines the monuments remain in the median of the highway guarding the two ends of the Henley Bridge.

The QEW was open to traffic as far as Niagara Falls by late 1939. In 1941, the road was extended between Niagara Falls and Fort Erie, although that section remained unpaved for the duration of World War II.

At the southern end of the QEW, the Peace Bridge to the United States had opened in 1927 and today carries more than four million vehicles a year. A park and monument dedicated to Alonzo Clark Mather, the determined proponent of the Peace Bridge, lie in the bridge's shadow in Fort Erie.

By the 1960s, traffic jams on the new highway had become a constant irritation. One source of frustration was the QEW lift bridge over the Welland Canal in Homer

The bulk carrier *Polsteam Mamry* passing through the Welland Canal under the Garden City Skyway on it's way to Lake Erie.

northeast of St. Catharines. Clearly, a new bridge was needed which would be wide enough for the traffic and high enough to allow the massive vessels using the Welland Canal to pass beneath.

The answer was the new six-lane Garden City Skyway. Completed in 1963, the structure stretches for more than two kilometres and rises 40 metres above the canal. Meanwhile, the old Homer Bridge remains in place as a piece of the QEW history.

Early Trails

Two separate pioneer trails led westward from the original colonial capital, Newark (Niagara-on-the-Lake), to the important town of Dundas at the head of Lake Ontario. Another trail ventured from the ferry dock at Queenston, near the foot of the escarpment, to Dundas, but this time by following the dry bench land below the cliffs of the Escarpment. It was known at the time as the Stoney Creek, Grimsby and Queenston Stone Road. In 1918, the road became one of the first roads in the province to be designated as a provincial highway, Highway 8 (now Regional Road 81). It is locally called York Road.

A little west of St. David's, the original roadway verges to the right and is known as Queenston Road. Upon passing beneath the Garden City Skyway, it returns to being Highway 81, and passes though St. Catharines along historic St. Paul Street. Emerging from St. Catharines, it becomes King Street and continues through vineyards and fruit lands, eventually succumbing to the urban sprawl of Stoney Creek and Hamilton.

Yet another vital pioneer trail was Lundy's Lane, connecting Lundy's Farm with the ferry docks at the foot of what is today known as Clifton Hill. Lundy's Lane, from the Portage Road to the Lundy's clearing, was made a public road in 1803.

THE CASTLES OF THE CUESTA
Niagara's Historic Mansions

Having some of Ontario's most spectacular settings, on rivers or perched atop high cliffs, it is little wonder that Niagara attracted some of Ontario's wealthiest people and their magnificent mansions. Here are a few.

Rodman Hall

Located on a hillside overlooking Twelve Mile Creek stands the castle known as Rodman Hall. Thomas Rodman Merritt was the youngest of the four sons of William Hamilton Merritt the industrialist who promoted the construction of the Welland Canal.

Thomas moved to St. Catharines in 1843 and opened a general store, partnering with James Benson. They soon expanded their operation to include a flour mill and the acquisition of a pair of ships to move their product to market.

In 1854, Thomas began the construction of this large Jacobean style mansion. Its floors were made of patterned inlaid hardwood and the ceilings were done with elaborate carvings and mouldings. Fireplaces boasted Italian marble. Inside, overlooking the grand hallway from the top of the stairs are massive stained-glass windows.

The former mansion of William Hamilton Merritt, promoter of the first Welland Canal, is now home to a local radio station.

In preparation for the home's construction, Merritt hired noted British gardener Samuel Richardson to design and lay out an extensive 2.9-hectare garden area with exotic trees and a hillside garden. Pine, maple, and black walnut trees still line the walkways. The garden is considered both an arboretum and a botanical garden.

The Hall remained in the family until 1959 when the City of St. Catharines acquired it. Following its purchase by Brock University, the building housed an extensive art gallery. When Brock could no longer afford the gallery, it was sold to a developer and the paintings and statues were removed. The Hall then became the Rodman Hall Inn, a 13-room boutique hotel and event venue managed by the equally historic Stone Mill Inn in Niagara Falls. The grounds of the Watson Arboretum remain available for the public to stroll and admire the gardens.

Oak Hill

While not as castle-like in appearance as Rodman Hall, Oak Hill is another Merritt historic home.

This was owned by William Hamilton Merritt himself. Built between 1858 and 1860, replacing his 1828 home which was destroyed by fire, this mansion combines Italianate and classical architectural styles. A prominent gable rises above the second floor while the tall narrow windows are capped with small pediments, as is the main door.

A lesser-known aspect of Merritt's life was his involvement with the Underground Railroad as a member of the Refugee Slaves' Friends Society. It is thought that a tunnel in the basement of the house may have allowed escaping slaves to enter the building from the Welland Canal, which followed Twelve Mile Creek.

Merritt died in 1862, willing the house to son Jedidiah. It remained in the family until 1923, when remaining members deeded the house to the City of St. Catharines. It became an inn in 1928. In 1938, the building became home to a radio station, a use it continues today as CKTB Radio at the east end of historic Yates Street.

Oak Hill is regarded as the gateway to the Yates Street heritage district. A historical plaque about Merritt stands beside the War Monument in Memorial Park beside the house. Oakhill Park, once part of the estate, lies opposite the house. From there, a path leads to the Merritt Trail in the valley. When it was created in 1933, it was described as "St. Catharines' most beautiful park." By the late 1970s, however, vandalism and lack of municipal care was taking its toll, and the park's beauty diminished. Its allure has been restored and it is once again a lovely idyll for visitors to the area.

The building forms a prominent landmark at the corner of Yates and St. Paul Street, the city's main thoroughfare.

Oak Hall

This magnificent castle, like Rodman Hall, is attributed to another of Canada's fabled opportunists, a multi-millionaire gold prospector named Harry Oakes.

A New Englander by birth, Harry Oakes started off in medical school in Syracuse, New York. But after only two years, he heard about the Klondike gold rush and off he went. Like most, he arrived at the gold fields to find the gold claims had already been staked and decided to give New Zealand a try. After finding no gold there, he tried the parched desert of California's Death Valley before heading to northern Ontario.

Finally, near Kirkland Lake, along with the Tough brothers, he at last hit the motherlode in the lake after which the town was named. Its value was beyond his wildest dreams. What had started out at 35 cents a share was soon worth $70 each. By 1921, Oakes was a millionaire.

Despite owning a mansion in Kirkland Lake, in 1924, he moved to a hilltop in Niagara Falls overlooking the great cataract and hired the architectural firm of Findlay and Fouls to build him a 37-room Tudor castle.

A noted philanthropist, Oakes donated land for an athletic field, still known today as Oakes Park, and land at the foot of Clifton Hill on which was built the Oakes Garden Theatre. He moved in 1934 to the tax-free haven of the Bahamas. In 1939, King George VI bestowed on him the title of Baronet, making him Sir Harry.

In 1943, his widow, Lady Eunice Oakes, donated Oak Hall to the Canadian government for use as a military hospital. In 1964, the Niagara Parks Commission acquired the castle, moving their own offices into it in 1982. They refurbished the grand hall, living room and dining room to their original condition and opened the historic home to the public. Oak Hall is on Portage Avenue at the south end of the city.

Oak Hall, built by Harry Oakes, gold prospector and millionaire, is currently used as offices by the Niagara Parks Commission.

Glencairn Hall

Overlooking the river and set back from the Parkway, 1.3 kilometres north of Queenston, the classical Greek style Glencairn Hall is one of the finer grand homes in Niagara, yet it is little known.

Designed by John Latshaw, it was built in 1832 for John Hamilton, who operated a number of ships on Lake Ontario.

Historic Rodman Hall is currently being used as a boutique hotel.

In 1866, William A. Thompson, president of the Erie and Niagara Railway bought the mansion expanding it and naming it Glencairn. In 1900, John D. Larkin, a soap factory owner from Buffalo, purchased the property as a home and picnic ground for his employees. He added a coach house, tearoom, and garden, using it mainly as a weekend retreat.

Now restored, the mansion contains 20 rooms with delicate cornices and eleven fireplaces. From the porch beneath the row of classical pillars, the view extends across the river from its 35-metre perch. Although the mansion lies down a lane called Larkin Road, the property is marked by a long dry-stone wall on the Parkway. The mansion today is A La Gallerie bed and breakfast.

Willowbank

Another grand home, Willowbank was built for Alexander Hamilton, the brother of John Hamilton, owner of neighbouring Glencairn Hall. Willowbank was completed in 1834. The estate remained in the family until 1934, when John Bright purchased the property which became part of Bright's wineries. It was then bought by the Missionary Sisters of Christian Charity, becoming the Appleton Boys School in 1982.

Three years later, a new buyer applied for a permit to alter the use of the property, but when that was not forthcoming, they applied for a demolition permit. Fortunately, the Friends of Willowbank, headed by Laura Dodson, rescued the home and converted it to the School of Restoration Arts, a use it continues to enjoy. Happily, its future seems assured thanks to an Ontario Heritage Trust easement and its designation as a National Historic Site of Canada. In 2014, the Prince of Wales (now King Charles III) added his patronage.

This remarkable structure, with its iconic plantation-style pillars overlooking the river, is best viewed from Queenston Street in the town, where the stone gates and overgrown lane indicate that its original entrance was from the river although today's main entrance lies on the Niagara Parkway alignment on the other side of the building. It is a school, not a tourist attraction, but it is a National Historic Site and easy to see from the road.

Glenview Mansion

Overlooking the Niagara Gorge from a high terrace sits one of the Parkway's other grand homes, the Glenview Mansion. It was built in 1870 in an Italianate style by John Drew, who was its first occupant. The building features a square plan with a pair of rear wings and a protected bay window capped off with a closed pediment.

The hall's next owner was John Ferguson. He was followed by Robert Peter Slater, a wealthy developer and later mayor of Niagara Falls. The 27-room building sits on what was originally a 32-hectare farm lot which stretched from River Road on the gorge to Victoria Avenue. He subdivided the estate into the residential lots that exist today. For a time during the 1950s it became the Whitehall Apartments and sported a coating of pink paint earning the nickname the Pink Palace.

In 2003, the City of Niagara Falls designated Glenview as a heritage structure; it is also registered on the list of Canada's Historic Places. It is situated at Buttrey Street and Terrace Avenue in the Silvertown district of the city. Today, the building is divided into apartments, known as the Whitehall Apartments, and is not a tourist attraction.

Bampfield Hall

Located just a block west of the River Road, on Zimmerman Avenue, Bampfield Hall is regarded as one Niagara Falls' most historic homes. The grand gothic style home was built by James Bampfield in 1875. Bampfield was involved in commercial developments along Queen Street in the downtown core of Niagara Falls. The building today is one of the area's many B&Bs.

Doran-Marshall Residence

Dominating the corner of River Road and Ellis Road, this is a Queen Anne style mansion with a prominent corner turret. Built in 1885, the mansion's cream-coloured brick and sweeping curved verandah make it one of the River Road's most visually stunning mansions. The original coach house still remains at the rear of the building. W.L. Doran was an early investor in several of the burgeoning city's many businesses.

Willowbank, one of Niagara's most historic and oldest mansions, is now a National Historic Site in Queenston.

Maplehurst

When completed in 1886, Maplehurst was considered "one of the most splendid homes between Toronto and Rochester."

Maplehurst, also known as the Keefer Mansion, is a 836-square metre red stone structure containing 3.6-metre ceilings and eight fireplaces. The mansion took just over a year to construct and included a new hot water heating system, indoor plumbing, and ornate extensive wood details. The roof is dominated by a widow's walk, a belvedere atop the roof.

However, the Keefers remained in the house for only eight years, as the taxes overwhelmed the family fortunes. Several tenants moved in and out during the following years until the 1930s, when it became a maternity hospital. It continued its role as a health care facility until 1999.

An application to demolish the mansion was denied by the City of Thorold, which purchased the property. In 2006, following three years of restorations, the building became the Keefer Mansion Inn and dining facility, although the future of these functions are uncertain at the time of this writing. Ironically, it also once more became part of the Keefer business empire, housing the offices of Keefer Developments Ltd.

The historic structure is considered a Thorold landmark. With its extensive grounds and stone fence, it sits on a prominent hilltop on St. David's Street West immediately west of Front Street North in Thorold.

Roselawn

This massive mansion is considered one of the area's loveliest homes. It was built in 1860 during the port's heyday by Levi Cornwall, a local merchant.

The McFarland house, built in the early 1800s, is the oldest property owned by the Niagara Parks Commission.

Centrally situated in the town, Roselawn is noted for its large garden and trees. In 1879, Lewis Carter acquired the house, expanding both house and garden. The building style is known as Second Empire, with elaborate rooflines and a high tower. It was formerly part of a 30-hectare farm adjacent to what was then the town's boundary.

A philanthropist, Carter hosted many politicians and dignitaries at his mansion. In 1866, he helped form a company to search for oil but instead tapped into a deposit of natural gas, which is why Roselawn became the first house in the village to be lit by gas.

The home's many notable features include the elaborate door on the east side with six panes of etched glass and a rose leaded glass window in the south wall. Interior features of particular interest include the detailed woodwork, decorative plaster work, ornate glass and the fireplaces.

The grand home passed through many hands before becoming the Port Colborne Club, an arts and cultural centre. The City of Port Colborne acquired the building, opening it to the public and inaugurating a theatre. Today, overlooking the grand hallway from the top of the stairs, are massive stained-glass windows. The theatre today runs the Showboat Festival in conjunction with the Lighthouse Festival in Port Dover. The mansion and its wide lawns sit on Fielden Avenue between Centre and Carter Streets. The building is open to the public during theatre season and for special events.

Lake House
Lake House is a familiar sight to motorists travelling along the QEW as they pass Jordan Harbour. It sits prominently on a bluff overlooking Lake Ontario and has an important history as one of the many stops on the Underground Railroad for Black slaves escaping from the United States to Canada. The building is said to be haunted by two resident ghosts, Elizabeth, a young girl, and "the captain," an old sailor. The building retains many of its original features, including beams, woodwork, three fireplaces, and brickwork. It became Lake House Restaurant in 2002.

Grandview Manor
As the prosperity of Niagara Falls grew, many grand homes were built along River Road overlooking the gorge. Among the more striking of these mansions is Grandview Manor at the corner of Eastwood Crescent. It was built in 1894 for Francis Shirriff who, with Thomas Bright, founded the Niagara Falls Wine Company (later renamed Brights Wines). Its Queen Anne style of architecture stands out along the road with a three-part window in the front gable and a Tuscan wrap-around porch, along with a prominent turret. The building now offers bed and breakfast accommodation.

Brown Homestead
Built in 1802 on a stretch of the Queenston pioneer trail, the Brown Homestead stands out in its current setting and has a grand tale to tell.

The area was settled around 1785 by Loyalist John Brown and his family. This historic site features the John Brown House, the oldest home in St. Catharines. It is a two-storey stone house built in 1802 which incorporates an earlier 1-1/2 storey house within its walls.

The property also includes the Norton Cabin (c. 1817). This historic cabin was built by Mohawk chief Teyoninhokarawen (John Norton), who commanded many of the Mohawk warriors who aided the British during the War of 1812. To save it from demolition, the simple wooden structure was moved from the Six Nations of the Grand River Territory at Brantford to the homestead grounds in 1997.

A member of the Palatine German settlement in New York State, Brown later sided with the Loyalists during the American Revolution, joining the legendary Butler's Rangers. As a Loyalist, he was forced to flee to Upper Canada in 1783 and received a 480-hectare grant of land on the busy pioneer Pelham Road. As all Loyalist settlers were required to do, he had to clear 0.8 hectares of land and construct a dwelling at least 20 by 16 feet.

Construction of the current building began in 1802. Following Brown's death in 1804, his son Adam converted the house to an inn and tavern to serve travellers on the busy pioneer Pelham Road. An unusual feature was a backroom bar known as a

Completed in 1886, Maplehurst in Thorold, was once described as "one of the most splendid homes between Toronto and Rochester."

birdcage bar. This type of bar consisted of a small square cubicle containing the supply of liquor, ale and crockery. These "birdcages" were an integral part of many early inns between 1700 and 1840, but few have survived. During alterations, the remains of the birdcage bar were found behind the Victorian wall near the fireplace in the parlour.

In 1858, the house was sold and became a private home. In 1978, a heritage consultant named Jon Jouppien acquired the property, and applied for a heritage designation for both the exterior and interior of the historic home. Both designations were granted in 1991. In 2015, the John Brown Heritage Foundation, founded by descendants of the original John Brown, acquired the property, naming it the John Brown Homestead.

The elegant brownstone structure is on Pelham Road opposite the entrance to the Short Hills Provincial Park.

Glasgow-Fortner House

Built around 1859, this three-storey mansion is described as "an excellent example of the Queen Anne revival style of domestic architecture." It displays an asymmetrical composition, with whimsical gables, dormers, porches, and balconies, and is dominated by its turret.

The house is located at 24 Burgar Street north of Division Street in Welland, and became a designated heritage property in 1985.

FORGOTTEN NIAGARA

Lost Villages and Ghost Towns

Niagara is a bustling region. Tourists flock to its casinos and attractions by the hundreds of thousands every year, and shoppers crowd into the outlet malls. Which is why it is curious that, in such a populated and busy area, there could be such things as ghost towns and vanished villages. But there are.

Clearly, these locations are not at all like the old mining boom towns of the Yukon, or the railway stops of the Prairies. They do, however, reflect the tides of changing technologies, transportation systems and government policies that have altered the landscape. Industries and businesses moved to better locations, leaving behind many of the earliest villages and towns. Amid today's population patterns, the legacy of these lost communities can still be found.

Ball's Falls

This early mill town with the rhyming name began as Glen Elgin in 1804, when brothers John and George Ball erected a two-storey grist mill atop the cascading waterfall on Twenty Mile Creek. A second falls tumbled further upstream, and here the Ball's placed a sawmill and woolen mill.

Water power from Twenty Mile Creek powered the mills which made Ball's Falls one of Niagara's earliest industrial centres. Built in 1804, the grist mill is now a museum.

A rusting railway track is all that remains of the Wainfleet Peat Bog's early peat extraction industry.

Between these two industrial sites, workers' cabins lined a network of lanes. Workers in the woolen mill, including local women who turned out goods including cashmeres, tweeds, and flannels, were accommodated in a five-storey boarding house.

For a time, Glen Elgin was the busiest industrial community in the growing Niagara area. Then the railways arrived; in 1853, the Great Western Railway laid its tracks well to the north of Glen Elgin, attracting new trackside communities like Jordan Station and Vineland Station. New industry located at trackside, leaving the village by the falls to wither.

Happily, the remains of Glen Elgin now lie preserved in the popular Ball's Falls Conservation Area. The ancient grist mill has become a museum, with the Ball family home standing nearby. Other historic structures, including a pioneer church and log cabin, were subsequently added to the site.

The site of the workers' homes has become a grassy lawn, while the road to the upper falls is now a trail. Along it, the stone foundation of the sawmill overlooks the upper falls, while the woolen mill and boarding have left precious little to see.

Visitors can pay to park at the conservation area office where they may pick up maps and information about the little ghost town along the river. The conservation area lies along Sixth Avenue east of Victoria Avenue.

St. John's West

It was to the banks of the Twelve Mile Creek nestled in the Short Hills that Benjamin Canby arrived in 1792 and built a small cabin. Although the waters of the creek were little more than a trickle, Canby successfully operated a sawmill. He was followed by John Darling, who added a grist mill. John married Canby's sister, building a small cabin for their home. When he added a newer home for his family, Canby's cabin became a school. Then, in 1817, Darling built Upper Canada's first iron foundry. By the 1840s, St. John's West was called "Upper Canada's leading industrial centre," which at its peak contained 150 inhabitants and five grist mills, three sawmills and a tannery along with general stores and churches.

Alas, the place succumbed to the same fate as Glen Elgin. The Welland Canal opened in 1828, and in 1853, the Great Western Railway bypassed the little hollow. The industries faded and the town stagnated. By the 1920s, it was being described as a "vanished village."

Like Ball's Falls, it retains a number of interesting vestiges of its glory days. Perhaps the most unusual is Canby's original cabin. Following his use of the place, it became Ontario's first public school. No bigger than a residential garage, it stands to this day, complete with a school bell atop a pole in front. It remains Ontario's smallest schoolhouse and hosts local school outings.

A few paces further along Orchard Hill Road from the school, a lane leads down a slope into the valley where the industries thrived. A solitary 19th-century house bears evidence that it may have also once been a grist mill. A few paces further along that lane, a small, preserved grist mill survives and is also used for educational outings.

The former main street, now called Holland Road, is partially lined with the foundations and cellar holes of the early homes and businesses, and in their midst is a small cemetery. From the back of the burial ground, a trail leads back down into the hollow.

Once marked by a historical marker on Holland Road, opposite the cemetery, was the St. John's tavern. In 1837, it witnessed the Raid on Short Hills during William Lyon Mackenzie's short-lived rebellion. When government troops took up residence in the hotel, rebels loyal to Mackenzie surrounded the place, taking the government force captive. Subsequently released, the government force captured the rebels and put them on trial. Among them was their local leader Samuel Chandler, who was banished to Van Diemen's Land (now Tasmania). An overgrown monument to Chandler lies along Orchard Hill Road, opposite the little schoolhouse.

The site of the school, and the industrial hollow, lies at the junction of Hollow Road and Orchard Road, south of Holland Road.

Homer

Little remains to be seen of the once-busy village of Homer. In 1795, a church was built along what was the main pioneer trail between Queenston and Burlington. The community later added a hotel, school and racetrack. The fourth version of the Welland

The former grist mill in the ghost town of St. John's West has been restored for educational purposes.

Canal opened through the village in 1926. In 1939, the new Queen Elizabeth Way carried a new four-lane thoroughfare along the earlier road through the town. As a result, old buildings were replaced by newer businesses to serve the travelling public.

Then, even that was replaced in 1963 by the soaring Garden City Skyway. While a few newer businesses have appeared along Homer's old road, only the Anglican cemetery and a few foundations remain from the early days of this forgotten place.

Beaver Dams

Beaver Dams is the oldest settlement in Thorold Township and contains the area's first township post office and other amenities. The Beaver Dams Methodist Church is likely Ontario's oldest surviving Methodist church to remain in continuous use. Built in 1832, the two-storey meeting house features a white clapboard exterior and two entrances at the front of the building. The church's architecture is similar in style to a New England Meeting House, with its simple rectangular shape and white clapboard siding. The church and burial ground are located on Marlatts Road.

Jordan Harbour

With its harbour and waterfalls upstream, the valley of Twenty Mile Creek was soon to attract arriving settlers. Large vessels could sail up the creek almost to Glen Elgin (Ball's Falls) to load wheat, oats, corn, and butter, as well as woolen goods from the woolen mill at Glen Elgin. But the buildup of silt across the mouth of the harbour and the construction of the Great Western Railway bridge in 1853 brought most shipping to a halt.

Then, with the incorporation of the new Jordan Harbour Company in 1899, shipping resumed and the harbour once more bustled with activity. In 1938, with the construction of the QEW, restaurants and motels were built and a conservation area was created to allow boating and fishing. The last vestige of the old community is today's Lake House Restaurant, sitting atop the bluff which overlooks the harbour.

Erie Beach Amusement Park

Anxious to escape the smothering smog in large American cities such as Cleveland and Buffalo, American tourists began seeking the cleaner air and uncrowded beaches of Ontario's Lake Erie shore. In 1885, a small picnic ground named Snake Hill Grove began to evolve into an amusement ground. Tourists from across the border arrived by either the Snake Hill and Pacific Railway from Fort Erie, or by steamer from across the lake.

By the 1920s, the park had grown and offered amusements such as camel rides, a roller coaster, bike races, a dance floor, and a 65-room hotel, complete with hot and cold running water. The swimming pool at the time was said to be the world's largest. Unlike much of Niagara in the early days, the park had electric lights.

In 1929, the American stock market crash ruined many businesses, including the Erie Beach Amusement Park. The owners of the nearby Crystal Beach Amusement Park bought the property and closed all the facilities. Most of the structures were removed or destroyed by fire. Only the casino (as dance halls were called at the time) remained standing. But, by 1976 the deteriorating shell was deemed unsafe, and it too was demolished.

These beachfront concrete pillars are all that remains of the abandoned Erie Beach Amusement Park in Fort Erie.

Today, the ghostly ruins of the park still linger in the growing forest. Old Lake Erie Beach Park lies within Waverly Beach Park, which is accessible from the west end of Lakeshore Road or from the parking lot at the foot of Helena Street. From each site, the new stone dust trail follows the beach, passing rotting steps and old foundations, including the remains of the wharf. A number of historic plaques describe the amusement grounds in its heyday, including one dedicated to the Niagara Movement, an initiative by a group of African Americans which lead to the start of the NAACP in the United States.

The newer amusement grounds, such as Canada's Wonderland, and the rise of the casinos in Niagara Falls spelled the end of the older park. The demand for beachfront condominiums became the inevitable fate of the park. Because the community is gated, visitors cannot even access the beach, and are confined to a much smaller shoreline park some distance way. The old main streets where popular summer treats and souvenirs once flourished now resemble a ghost town.

Niagara Circles

Look on any street map or Google satellite view of Niagara-on-the-Lake, Niagara Falls or Crystal Beach to see something unusual. Amid the usual grid layout of the town are streets which form a circular pattern. These were created by a cultural phenomenon known as the Chautauqua Movement. The aims of the movement were to bring the arts and religious services to people who would not otherwise have access to them.

The Niagara region was once host to four separate meeting grounds which operated on the Chautauqua principle. The events took place in a large auditorium. Members built cottages in a circle around the auditorium, and hotels housed those without private places. An amusement park evolved as well. By the 1930s, the operation had ended, and the hotels burned. Grimsby Park has survived today as a distinctive historic area, with a number of the cottages now designated as individual heritage properties. These gaily painted homes with gabled porches are now within Grimsby's urban boundary.

Crystal Beach Amusement Park

This popular destination operated from 1888 until 1989. Crystal Beach drew most of its visitors from American cities, many arriving daily on the steamer *Canadiana*. The opening of the Queen Elizabeth Way, a four-lane highway from Toronto, drew more Canadians in the park's later years. But the ballrooms, bathhouses, and big band sounds did not last forever.

The Merriton Tunnel, also known as the Blue Ghost Tunnel, is an abandoned Grand Trunk Railway tunnel running under the Welland Canal.

Three other lesser-known meeting grounds, known as Chautauquas, operated in Niagara as well: at Niagara-on-the-Lake, Niagara Falls and Crystal Beach. At each site, the circular arrangements of the streets survive and reflect this early phenomenon, although original structures do not. While evidence of these grounds is gone, a heritage district in Grimsby known as Grimsby Park continues to display early Chautauqua cottages and relics from the meeting camp as well.

The Methodist camp meeting grounds in Crystal Beach opened in 1888 modelled upon the Chautauqua site in New York State. When the amusements closed, the park became a gated community. However, the circular street pattern remains in place, although no buildings from the days of the campgrounds have survived. Queens Circle, the site today of landscaped grounds and a seasonal farmers' market, encloses the site of the auditorium, while an outer circle is now Lincoln Road. The circular streets

The historic Beaverdams Church in the hamlet of Beaver Dams.

lie at the north end of the Derby Road business district.

Niagara-on-the-Lake enjoyed its own Chautauqua-style assembly as well. In 1887, the Chautauquans established an assembly ground to the north of the town's then limits, on the shore of Lake Ontario. Typically, they laid out a circular street pattern, in the centre of which was the three-storey Hotel Chautauqua and a 3,000 seat auditorium. Visitors arrived by steamer from Toronto or by rail along a spur line from the Michigan Central Railroad line. Besides the religious services, visitors could enjoy poetry, lectures, music and theatre.

In 1909, the hotel burned, and the finances of the assembly faltered. Tourists began to look elsewhere for their amusements. By the 1920s, the lands were being subdivided for new homes. Today, the sole evidence of the old meeting ground lies in the configuration of Circle Street, and the side streets which radiate from it. Some of those side streets bear names like Shakespeare and Wesley, which bespeak the nature of the Chautauquans. At the southwest side of the circle, a small treed area and playground retains the name Chautauqua Park.

In 1885, the Niagara Falls International Camp Meeting Association opened their meeting grounds, which was called Wesley Park. The site was to be a major campground and summer resort based on the Chautauqua concept. The grounds took in 80 hectares and the property was laid out in circles, where members would erect their cottages and homes. A 20-hectare parcel was set aside for forest lands.

The grounds were enclosed by today's Simcoe Street, River Road, Roberts Street, and Stanley Avenue, and is now known as the Epworth neighbourhood. On the property were more than 900 cottages on lots 20 metres wide by 40 metres long. The grounds could also boast their own dedicated post office and railway station, as well as access to the base of the nearby Niagara Gorge via Pelly's staircase.

By 1887, the camp meetings had largely faded out and the lots were sold off. The uses of the auditorium site today include a dog training academy, a school and daycare centre. The circular street configuration of the Niagara Falls Chautauqua camp survives and lies between Victoria Street and Palmer Avenue.

Haunted Niagara

For avid ghost hunters, Niagara has plenty of locations said to enjoy the company of visitors who come and go all too quietly. Many of the area's haunted places have been around for a long time, often after experiencing many tragic departures.

Glenview Mansion in the Silvertown neighbourhood of Niagara Falls is the subject of stories about two murders that occurred outside the mansion. The spirits of the victims are said to still linger. One murder involved the story of a fraudulent effort to sell the mansion by someone who didn't own it. Another murder story concerns a couple who attended a party at Glenview. As they were waiting for their horse-drawn carriage, they were attacked and killed. Witnesses have claimed to see the bloody carriage on the driveway.

One of Niagara's most visited historic sites is Fort George. Even though the stone powder magazine is the only original building, the rest were all reconstructed or replicated during the 1930s, many paranormalists believe that the fort is one of the most haunted places in Niagara.

Given its military history, and the many deaths that occurred there during the War of 1812 when the fort changed hands several times, it would make sense that these spectres would be those of the military men or possibly their family members.

Not too surprisingly, ghost tours of this site have become among the more popular in Niagara. Visitors have claimed to have seen shadowy figures in the tunnel between the buildings. Staff report figures that seem to appear and vanish on the second floor of the blockhouse.

This historic town has more than its share of haunted hotels. One is the Olde Angel Inn. The phantom in this case is purportedly that of a Canadian militia officer from the War of 1812 who roams the halls and rooms, seeking his lost lover. Guests have reported their shoes and other objects mysteriously being moved.

Yet another popular historic Niagara-on-the-Lake hotel is the Prince of Wales Inn. Here, the rooms are supposedly haunted by a woman named Molly Maguire who was staying in room 207 awaiting the return of her soldier husband, when she was killed by an American soldier. The lights in her old room are said to sometimes go on and off without the assistance of a human hand.

Another haunted building in the town, known now as the Brockamour Manor, is a grand home built by Captain John Powell in 1809. It is one of the few to have escaped the flames of the Americans in 1813. It was also known as the Powell House. Powell's sister-in-law, Sophia, was a frequent guest as was General Isaac Brock. No sooner had the two become secretly engaged (hence the name "Brock amour") when Brock lost his life at the Battle of Queenston Heights. Devastated, Sophia stayed in the house until she died and, according to some accounts, possibly after that as well.

Another supposedly haunted fort is Fort Erie. The site of bloody fighting during the War of 1812, it witnessed many deaths. Amongst the reconstructed buildings, visitors have been said to see soldiers wandering the halls. One of them has no hands, the other is lacking his head. In addition to these ghastly apparitions is the evidence that Captain Kingsley of the 8th Regiment may not entirely have vacated the premises. Long bedridden, he died of fever and other ailments. In the replica of his room today, visitors can experience disrupted sheets, footsteps and windows which mysteriously open and shut on their own. All of this in a fort with no original buildings.

In addition to the buildings, two Niagara tunnels are said to be the location of paranormal phenomena. One, situated on the

The screaming tunnel near Thorold is said to be haunted by the ghost of a young girl who tragically burned to death there.

Bruce Trail, basically a stone-lined drainage tunnel and farm carriageway beneath the railway tracks, is known as the Screaming Tunnel. A young girl was said to have been fatally set on fire by her deranged father and fled into the tunnel, where she perished. Since then, a lit match is said to extinguish itself as midnight approaches. The tunnel lies beside Warner Road, across from the Perridiso Estate Winery.

Then there is the Blue Ghost Tunnel, an abandoned railway tunnel created by the Great Western Railway in 1876, beneath the Welland Canal. The tunnel was cut as a ditch at first and then roofed over before the canal was finished. After 40 years, the Grand Trunk Railway built a bridge over the canal and abandoned the section of its line through the tunnel.

Originally called the Merritton Tunnel, it earned the "Blue Ghost Tunnel" name when an early ghost hunter photographed what he claimed was a blue mist in the shape of a human. One theory for the ghostly shape comes from the fate of the crew members of two trains which collided head-on near the tunnel in 1903. Although both engineers survived the calamity, the two firemen died and are said to haunt the cold and damp ditch in the form of orbs or wisps of mist.

Other theories about what haunts the tunnel include workmen killed during construction or unhappy spirits from a nearby cemetery which was flooded to accommodate the new canal. The stone arch tunnel runs for 280 metres and can be slippery underfoot, much of its length now flooded. While plywood has been slapped over the entrance, vandals have regularly cracked it open to get in. Or are the ghosts possibly trying to get out?

Ghost in the Power Station

Completed in 1904, later decommissioned, and now a new Niagara tourist attraction, the Niagara Parks Power Station may have a ghost or two. Night shift workers often claim to see a well-dressed woman walking around the plant. The plant was originally called the William Birch Rankine Power Station, after the man who promoted the need for the electric facility. He married a much younger woman, Annette Norton, a wealthy New Yorker. Sadly, the marriage was short-lived, as Rankine died during their honeymoon. The distraught Annette returned to New York, and 16 years later an unconfirmed report suggested she committed suicide by jumping from the Queensboro Bridge.

Ghost hunters, using the latest ghost hunting technology, claim to have contacted spirits within the plant. Could one of them be the unfortunate Annette trying to return to her deceased husband, or possibly the spirits of workers who died during the plant's construction?

Drummond Hill Cemetery

Hundreds of soldiers died here in the Battle of Lundy's Lane, one of the deadliest battles of the War of 1812. Some visitors have claimed to see amid the graves shadowy spectres rising from behind the headstones and feeling a cold draft on their necks.

A monument honours British soldiers buried in the Drummond Hill Cemetery in Niagara Falls. It is said to be guarded by the spirits of the dead soldiers.

DAY TRIPS AND EXPLORATIONS — NIAGARA OUT OF DOORS

NATURE'S WONDERS
Niagara's Conservation Areas

Ontario's conservation movement began in the late 1940s. Something needed to be done to prevent the perpetual spring floods that inundated many of Ontario's riverside towns. In addition, farming practices had denuded much of the fertility of the sandy soils around the province, turning farmland into desert landscapes.

In 1942, the Ontario government tasked Arthur Herbert Richardson with the job of conducting a survey of the Ganaraska River watershed. After surveying the area, he recommended that a system of conservation authorities, modelled after the Tennessee Valley Authority in the United States, be established throughout the province which would include the municipalities within a given watershed. Methods of improving flood control and erosion mitigation would be their priorities.

There were some side benefits that came with the plan. Water control often meant constructing a series of control dams which would offer recreation opportunities. These dams would sometimes coincide with mill ponds and mills, and these became sites of heritage preservation, such as at Ball's Falls Conservation Area near Vineland. Conservation authorities would also be responsible for

The lower falls at Ball's Falls is one of two which powered the mills in this early industrial village.

reviewing development plans for potential flooding risks and wetland and wildlife protection.

Following his report, Richardson became Ontario's first conservation engineer. The Conservation Authorities Act of 1946 enabled those municipalities within watersheds to share the cost of flood control and sound soil management. In 1959, the Niagara Peninsula Conservation Authority came into existence and now manages 41 conservation areas.

Since its start, the NPCA has assembled more than 2,800 hectares of land for visitors to explore. These range from soggy bogs to manicured picnic grounds and rare Carolinian forests. Many of them contain heritage buildings as well.

Wainfleet Bog Conservation Area

A bog may not sound like an appealing place to explore, but the Wainfleet peat bog, west of Port Colborne, is an exception. The bog began to form following the retreat of the last glacier 20,000 years ago, causing meltwater to form a pond behind the adjacent Onondaga Escarpment. This stagnant open-water area created a habitat for rare plants and animals which could withstand the acidic and low-nutrient conditions. As these plants died and accumulated, peat was created. After originally covering more than 20,000 hectares along the Lake Erie shore between Port Colborne and the Grand River, drainage for farmlands and for peat extraction shrank its area to a mere 1,400 hectares.

In 1894, peat extraction in Ontario began when the Ontario Peat Company purchased 800 hectares of the bog. During the summers, labourers cut the peat into squares and loaded them onto carts, which were pulled along a narrow-gauge rail track to the Atkinson and Dunn factory at the edge of the bog, where the peat was processed. The Ontario Peat Company took over the operation until operations ceased in the 1980s. Then the Ontario Ministry of Natural Resources assumed stewardship of 800 hectares of the bog.

Despite the diminution of the area of the bog, it remains the largest such bog in southern Ontario. It retains many distinctive flora and fauna and is one of the few surviving habitats of the Massassauga Rattlesnake south of Georgian Bay.

Although lightly used, the bog does have a small trail system. The route generally follows the old railway bed from the parking lot to a "T" junction of trails within the dense growth. Along the trail the hikers may find themselves walking on old rusting rails atop rotting wooden ties. Years ago, this author came upon deteriorating rail cars, and the rusting relic of one of the locomotives. All of these have since been removed. The parking lot for the conservation area lies at the north end of Erie Peat Road which leads from Highway 3 west of Port Colborne.

Wainfleet Wetlands Conservation Area

Separate from the larger bog, and much drier, this conservation area is the remains

The ancient Comfort Maple in Pelham is over 400 years old.

of a limestone quarry. The site offers opportunities to view some of the rare fossils which lie at the surface. The former site of an aggregate quarry, the site also contains two ponds from that early operation. To reach this unusual geological site, take Quarry Road south from Highway 3, west of Port Colborne. The bedrock here contains many varieties of fossils and a ridge of uplifted rock resulting from an ancient earthquake. The quarry is a poplar location for kayakers. Parking for the quarry is on Quarry Road, marked by the sign for the Gord Harry Trail.

Ball's Falls Conservation Area

This site, more fully described under the "Ghost Towns" section of this book, is an educational experience with its large interpretation centre and riverside trails. It hosts student outings for the local youth. There is paid parking at the centre from which trails follow the river to its waterfalls and to the sites of the vanished mill town. The 1804 mill houses a museum. The area lies on Sixth Avenue east of Victoria Avenue.

Comfort Maple Conservation Area

This small conservation area was created to protect what is considered to be Canada's oldest maple tree. Some estimates suggest that the tree was three centuries old by the time the War of 1812 broke out. With a few benches and interpretative plaques, the tree is located on Metler Road near Pelham. The massive maple stands on land that was donated to the conservation authority in 1961 by the pioneering Comfort family to preserve this remarkable specimen. It was designated as a Heritage Tree of Ontario in 2000. The tree measures 24.5 metres in height, with a circumference of 38 metres.

The Comfort Maple, however, has a rival for the distinction of being the oldest tree. The Allanburg Oak is a magnificent white oak identified by members of the community as an important part of their neighbourhood heritage. Estimates put its age as dating back to 1650. Although it does not lie in a conservation area, this mammoth oak tree has been assessed by the Niagara Peninsula Conservation Authority to be in excellent condition and is on the Honour Roll of Ontario Trees. The tree is clearly visible behind 2364 Centre Street in Allanburg.

Jordan Harbour Conservation Area

Jordan Harbour is protected as an Area of Natural and Scientific Interest (ANSI) and contains a variety of unique wildlife and tree species that are rarely seen elsewhere in the peninsula. This Provincially Significant Wetland is on the south shore of Lake Ontario at the estuary of Twenty Mile Creek. The kilometre-wide harbour offers a public launching dock for non-motorized watercraft and was once the site of a busy fishing village. At the head of the harbour, the tracks of the CN Rail line cross the waterway on a long bridge, beside which are the stone piers of the railway's original bridge. The park is located off South Service Road, east of Victoria Avenue.

The wreckage of *La Grande Hermine*, once a floating restaurant, was a familiar site in Jordan Harbor for decades. Sadly, the masts have now collapsed and the old ship is quickly deteriorating.

Niagara's little-known Short Hills Provincial Park offers stunning scenery and tranquil trails.

Louth Conservation Area

Located southwest of St. Catharines, this 36-hectare parcel of land on Sixteen Mile Creek was purchased in 1973. It contains a portion of the Niagara Escarpment and provides access to the Bruce Trail. Its trails reveal ancient and unusual rock formations and two waterfalls. Access is via Staff Avenue north of Pelham Road.

Mountainview Conservation Area

This 24-hectare parcel of Carolinian forest offers shady hiking trails with views from the top of the escarpment and provides important habitat for several species of animals. Its geological highlights include exposed dolostone rock, many bedrock fractures, and the eroded talus slopes. Access is from Mountainview Road, south of the QEW.

Rockway Conservation Area

This park's two waterfalls plunge into one of the escarpment's more stunning gorges, a steep cleft in the rock wall which exposes many of the escarpment's geological layers. The trail along Fifteen Mile Creek valley leads through mature stands of basswood, sugar maple, black walnut, and sycamore trees.

The spectacular waterfalls plunge from heights of 19.5 metres, and 12.2 metres, respectively, surging over a series of ridges and rapids. The upper waterfall is right beside the road at the Rockway Community Centre on Regional Road 69, while the lower falls are accessible along some precipitous trails lower down the valley. A small parking lot on Ninth Street accesses the trail system, which includes the Bruce Trail.

St. John's Conservation Area

This shady and rolling park lies in the St. John's Valley, close to the ghost town of St. John's West and not far from Short Hills Provincial Park. St. John's is also known for bird watching and contains a pond for fishing enthusiasts. Four trails lead through the site. Access is from Hollow Road north of Fonthill.

Virgil Dam and Reservoir Conservation Area

This small area rings a reservoir above the Virgil Dam on Four Mile Creek in Niagara-on-the-Lake.

Rock falls make this section of the Bruce Trail through the Woodend Conservation Area a challenge for hikers.

Woodend Conservation Area

Although small at 40 hectares, the area has stunning views from the brink of the escarpment and provides educational sessions in a historic 1931 house, now the Woodend Environmental Centre. The property was originally owned by Loyalist pioneer Peter Lampman and covered 400 hectares. Access is from Taylor Road south of Glendale Avenue in St. Catharines, or from the Bruce Trail. Parking is along Taylor Road.

Cave Springs Conservation Area

Access to this area is primarily from the Bruce Trail. The trail is accessible from a parking area on Quarry Road, south from Regional Road 81 and east of Beamsville. It may be one the area's most intriguing lands. In addition to its maple forest and views over the farmlands below, it is alleged to contain an underground lake, an ice cave, and unexplained rock carvings.

CULTIVATED BEAUTY
Niagara's Formal Gardens

Among Niagara's many claims to fame are its gardens, in particular those along the Niagara Parkway. The landscaping along this scenic drive has been the purview of the Niagara Parks Commission since its creation in 1885.

Just outside Niagara-on-the-Lake, a natural area called Paradise Grove Oak Savannah Restoration Area preserves ancient oaks which were saplings centuries before the War of 1812. The grove includes a rare remnant of the tall grass prairies once common in southern Ontario. The 26-hectare grove sits just south of John Street in Niagara-on-the-Lake, on the bank of the Niagara River. Here, the Niagara Parks Commission has worked to restore the oak forest and the savannah, as well as removing invasive species. As with the famous black oak savannah in Toronto's High Park, this ecosystem also requires regular controlled burns to help with regeneration.

No visit to Niagara is complete without a stop at the Botanical Gardens. Niagara Parks' Botanical Gardens features 40-hectares of award-winning landscapes, complemented by vibrant seasonal

Queen Victoria Place is an historic building now housing a gift shop and restaurant.

A short distance from the crowds and cacophony of Niagara Falls, the Dufferin Islands Park, opposite the Old Scow Lookout, offers a tranquil and beautiful retreat.

blooms and lush, overflowing gardens. The garden's trails wind through the arboretum with its wide variety of tree species. The Victorian rose garden shows off 2,400 roses of various types. More than 80,000 plants begin their lives in the gardens' greenhouse before being planted in the garden. All are tended to by the students at the Niagara Parks School of Horticulture housed in a large historic house on the grounds. An adjacent building is a former railway station which once served the Niagara Falls Park and River Railway. The gardens have been part of the acclaimed Niagara Garden Trail since 1990.

Niagara Parks Butterfly Conservatory

Located adjacent to the Botanical Garden, the Niagara Parks Butterfly Conservatory is home to 2,000 butterflies of 45 different species. They flit about the patrons along the pathways, which wind through an indoor rainforest and past ponds and waterfalls. At the start of the path system, a small theatre features videos about the life of the insect and the work of the conservatory.

Queen Victoria Park

In 1885, the Ontario Government created the Niagara Parks Commission. The commission began to landscape a 60-hectare

The beautiful Butterfly Conservatory is home to more than 45 species of butterflies.

The historic Walker Arboretum and Botanical Garden at Rodman Hall Boutique Hotel in St. Catharines remain open to the public.

parcel with trees and flower beds and opened the area as Queen Victoria Park in 1888. Along its walkways are rock gardens, hanging baskets and a hybrid tea rose garden. The colours of spring begin with the blooming of 500,000 daffodils, followed by the tulips and magnolia blossoms. Summer features annual bedded plants straight from the Niagara Parks greenhouse. Wintertime features a Christmas lights festival, a New Year's Eve concert and fireworks, while the ice formations along the river created by the freezing mist from the falls are a long-visited natural wonderland.

Considered the gateway to Queen Victoria Park, the spectacular Oakes Garden Theatre, opened in 1937, is one of the fall's more attractive features. Designers took

Niagara Parks Floral Showhouse

Established in the 1960s, adjacent to the Niagara Power Station, the Niagara Parks Floral Showhouse presents an indoor tropical oasis of orchids, succulents, and various tropical plants. Outside the building, summertime provides a fragrance garden with walkways winding throughout and includes an Artist's Garden.

Dufferin Islands

As part of its initial mandate, the Niagara Parks Commission acquired Clark Islands immediately south of the Toronto Power Station in 1887. The site of an early mill in the 1790s, by 1820, the site had become one of the area's first tourist attractions with its Burning Springs, a natural gas outlet. Its owner would ignite the gas to the delight and amazement of the tourists. In 1902, when the Ontario Power Company began diverting water from the Niagara River for its new power plant, the Parks Commission struck a deal to convert the site into a more natural environment, preserving the trees and creating walkways around artificial islands. The grounds are popular with picnickers, hikers and birdwatchers. The tranquility here is in sharp contrast to the bustle around the falls and Clifton Hill just a short distance away.

Garden City, St. Catharines

St. Catharines, called the Garden City, contains some of Niagara's loveliest parks and gardens. One of those is Montebello Park. Montebello Park was designed in 1887 by Frederick Law Olmstead, the founding

advantage of the slope and curvature of the terrain to create curved seating under a wraparound wooden pagoda. Decorative iron gates, Queenston limestone edging, stone gardens, water features, ponds and bordering shrubs have been meticulously integrated to the formal garden design. From the terraces in the garden, views extend across the river to both sets of falls. Despite its name, the Oakes Garden Theatre does not host regular performances.

father of landscape architecture in the United States and one of the designers of Central Park in New York City. Montebello Park contains a pavilion, playground equipment, and a rose garden. The park is located at the corner of Ontario and Lake Streets.

Another renowned St. Catharines park is Lakeside Park. Created in conjunction with the Niagara, St. Catharines and Toronto Railway, this long-established park, located in Port Dalhousie, has hosted travellers arriving by rail and from across the lake by steamer. While many were coming for the beaches, others of the younger set were anxious to ride the famous Looff carousel. The historic carousel was hand-carved by Charles I.D. Looff from 1898 to 1905. It was relocated from a park in Scarborough to Lakeside Park in 1921 and became an instant attraction. Aside from upgrades since then, it has remained in use. And it still costs only a nickel to ride. It remains one of nine antique hand-carved carousels still operating in Canada. The lion is the only one of five original Looff lions still existing in North America and the only one with its head turned outward toward the onlookers.

Jaycee Gardens Park contains a thoughtfully decorated memorial to the memory of Kristen French, a teenage girl who was murdered in 1995. The granite marker sits in the Green Ribbon Memorial Park inside Jaycee Gardens. The entrance to the park, which is adjacent to Royal Henley Park, lies on Ontario Street near Port Dalhousie in St. Catharines. Aside from the touching memorial, Jaycee Gardens also consists of about eight hectares of stunning landscapes of many different flowers, trees and lush green grass.

Walker Botanical Garden and Arboretum

St. Catharines has its own botanical garden, the Walker arboretum at the historic Rodman Hall mansion. In 1856, Thomas Rodman Merritt, son of canal builder William Hamilton Merritt, built a magnificent house overlooking Twelve Mile Creek. He called it Rodman Hall.

To landscape his eight hectares, Merritt hired an English landscaper named Samuel Richardson. On the hillside leading down to Twelve Mile Creek, Richardson laid out a garden featuring exotic trees, fountains, borders and a terraced lawn and orchard. With its wide variety of trees, it is often referred to as the Walker Arboretum. Maintenance of the grounds has been shared between Brock University and the City of St. Catharines. In 2022, the arboretum grounds were sold to a developer but remain open to the public. The grand home is now a boutique hotel and event venue.

Part of the 2,400 roses on display at the Niagara Parks Botanical Garden Victorian rose garden.

HAPPY TRAILS

Niagara's Walking and Hiking Trails

Despite its urban sprawl, Niagara offers a number of trails to hike, bike, and even gallop. Among the oldest and best known is the famous Bruce Trail.

Bruce Trail

In 1959, inspired by the success of the Appalachian Trail in the eastern United States, the Federation of Ontario Naturalists convened a meeting to create a similar hiking trail in the province which would allow the public to enjoy the flora, the fauna, the geological oddities, and the stunning views and natural wonders that line the 725-kilometre-long Niagara Escarpment from Queenston to Tobermory.

But getting access to a continuous route along the ridge was not easy. Most of the land was privately owned, and not all of the owners relished the prospect of strangers wandering through their backyards. Over the following years, nine regional clubs were formed and volunteers went, literally, door-to-door, talking to farmers, home owners and local municipalities, touting the aims and benefits of a hiking trail. This finally led to the establishment of the Bruce Trail Conservancy in 1963. In 1967, Canada's

Beautiful Sherman Falls in Hamilton lies along the Bruce Trail on the Niagara Escarpment.

The precipitous gorge at Rockway Falls, just east of Ball's Falls.

Centennial year, the first iteration of the trail opened, with the revealing of a stone cairn in Queenston Heights Park to mark the trail's southern terminus.

Today, the 900-kilometre Bruce Trail, along with 450 kilometres of side trails, is world-famous along with the 725 kilometre-long Niagara Escarpment, now a designated UNESCO Biosphere Reserve. The Niagara portion of the trail extends more than 80 kilometre from Queenston Heights Park to Forty Mile Creek. Along the Niagara section, the main trail gives access to 17 different side trails.

The trail begins at the southern cairn and crosses the parking lot for Queenston Heights Park, then leads though a variety of steep forest paths and roadside routes.

Along the way, it passes by Niagara's iconic vineyards before continuing through the Screaming Tunnel. Supposedly, this tunnel, originally built as a drainage tunnel beneath the railway tracks, became a haunting legend years ago after a young girl burned to death within it. The screams of the tragic victim can be heard, it is said, and whenever a visitor attempts to light a match within it around the midnight hour, the flame suddenly goes out.

The trail then enters the Woodend Conservation Area. From the cliff known as St. Anthony's Nose, wide vistas extend over the lands below the cliffs. After passing a golf course, the trail encounters the ruins of the locks and piers of the third Welland canal. The trail follows the bank of the old canal for about one kilometre to Glendale Avenue. This segment of the canal was where Locks 14 through 17 ascended the escarpment and are the only location at which the public may view the ruins of Canal 3.

After passing through the streets of St. Catharines to Moodie Lake, the trail reaches one of this section's most historic locations, the DeCew House and the headquarters of Lieutenant James FitzGibbon. This was the point which Laura Secord reached on her famous trek during the War of 1812, to warn FitzGibbon of a pending American assault on Beaver Dams. He used Secord's revelation to thwart the invading American forces. Fittingly, here the Bruce Trail connects with the Laura Secord Legacy Trail.

A short distance later, the trail comes to the historic and photogenic Morningstar Mill and Museum. Wilson Morningstar built his stone flour mill here in 1872. A small hamlet grew around the site while the former family home rests on a hill above the mill pond. The mill remained in use following his death in 1933. In 1994, the family deeded both house and mill to the City of St. Catharines which now operates it as a museum. After a few more kilometres, past the mill, the trail enters the scenic Short Hills Provincial Park, with access to the seven trails in that lush glade.

The next sight along the trail is Rockway Falls and its deep scenic gorge. Then the trail leads through forest and field to the Louth Conservation Area and the Louth Falls. From the parking lot for the conservation area, the trail takes to the roads and then though more woodland to the Eighteen Mile Creek Falls. A few more kilometres of wooded walking trails lead to the valley of the Twenty Mile Creek and the Ball's Falls Conservation Area. Here it encounters the historic ghost town of Ball's Falls, with its mill museum and pioneer village.

From there, the trail again takes hikers along farm lanes, through the forests of the Cave Springs Conservation Area, and then past Thirty Mile Creek Falls. Following the clifftops, the trail leads to Forty Mile Creek and the 80-kilometre mark. The Beamer Memorial Conservation Area, above the town of Grimsby, marks the end of the Niagara Portion.

An essential accompaniment for hiking the Bruce Trail is the *Bruce Trail Reference Maps & Trail Guide*. It provides details of the trail and maps, and guides to the many side trails as well. It is updated on a regular basis.

Side Trails

Due to the enormous popularity of the Bruce Trail and its economic impact on the surrounding communities and businesses, many side trails have been opened and lead from the Bruce Trail like branches from the trunk of a tree. Most are under the auspices of the Bruce Trail Conservancy, although there are links to other side trails created by local municipalities and community groups.

General Brock Side Trail

This 12.4-kilometre route leads down the rugged slope of the escarpment from the Trailhead Cairn in Queenston Heights Park to the historic village of Queenston. Various historic sites come into view along it, including the abandoned roadbed of the Niagara Falls Park and River Railway, which lasted from the 1890s to the 1930s.

Other important features include the St. Saviour's Church (1879) and the Stone Cottage. After following some of Queenston's scenic streets, the trail joins up with the Niagara River Recreation Trail leading along the Niagara River into Niagara-on-the-Lake. This latter trail is multi-use, paved, and provides picnicking opportunities, seating and views of the placid river that runs beside it.

Bert Lowe Side Trail

This 12-kilometre loop allows hikers to view some of the Welland Canal's more significant features. After heading south from the main Bruce Trail at the 19-kilometre mark, it follows the banks of the canal past the engineering marvel of the Twin Flight Locks to Allanburg, where it swings back to

the north. It then follows the shore of Lake Gibson, a reservoir created for the DeCew Falls Generating Stations. It rejoins the main trial at the DeCew House.

Laura Secord Legacy Trail

This 32-kilometre trail generally follows the route taken by Secord from her house in Queenston to the headquarters of Lieutenant James FitzGibbon to warn him of a pending

The Morningstar Mills Historic Site is a highlight on the Bruce Trail, southwest of St. Catharines.

American attack. She passed through forests and rocky cliffs until, in the latter portion of it, she was joined by a group of First Nations warriors who served as her guides.

While large portions of that route have today become incorporated into highways and side streets, portions of it still offer the rugged wooded terrain which confronted her on her difficult trek. The trail system, also links with the Merritt Trail in St. Catharines and the Bruce Trail at DeCew Falls.

The trail is divided into five easy-to-walk stages, some of which follow the Bruce Trail. Specific directions can be found online at friendsoflaurasecord.com.

Another side trail, the DeCew Loop

Trail, provides a 4-kilometre loop which leads past the waterfalls at the Morningstar Mill historic site and accesses two lower curtain-style falls on the creek.

Trails of the Niagara Glen

The four kilometres of trails in the Niagara Glen reserve are unlike any other in the Niagara area. With its Carolinian forests and unusual rock formations, the glen has been a designated Nature Reserve since 1992.

The trails begin at the Niagara Glen Nature Centre on the Niagara Parkway, where background information and maps are available, as well as washrooms and souvenirs. Then, after an easy stroll across the grassy picnic grounds to the lip of the escarpment, things get interesting.

Here the trail descends a 40-metre high metal staircase to the Main Trail, a loop around the perimeter of the glen. From it, side trails lead to the River Trail and the Cliffside Trail, where the hiker walks beneath the sheer rock wall of the escarpment face.

The Cliffside Trail leads to the Eddy Trail. Although it is less than 250 metres long, this section wanders around and under massive boulders wrenched from the cliffs by erosion and freeze-thaw forces. These elements have broken the massive blocks of rock from the cliff and have done so for more than 10,000 years.

Longer and more dramatic, the River Trail descends down to the water's edge, where the mighty rapids of the gorge leap and crash in awe-inspiring mountains

The boardwalk makes it easy to visit White Water Walk in early fall.

of water. These are often considered the mightiest rapids in the world, as they foam and rush past at almost 50 kph. The standing waves and rapids soar higher than the riverbank itself. Two shorter trails, the Terrace Trail and the Trillium Trail, guide the hiker past more of the glen's weird and wonderful rock formations, including one evocatively known as the Devil's Arch.

From the north end of the Main Loop, a 1.9-kilometre trail takes hikers to one of the glen's highlights, a view of the Whirlpool.

Massive sheer boulders on the Bouldering Trail, a side trail from the Main Loop Trail, have become popular with boulder climbers (known as bouldering, for which a permit is required), and requires much the same skills and equipment as rock climbing.

While some portions of the trail system are fine for less experienced hikers, most fall into a moderate or difficult classification; details are available in the Niagara Glen Nature Centre.

White Water Walk

Although it is not a nature trail, the White Water Walk is an attraction that provides a less strenuous way to experience the might of the rapids in the gorge. Access is by way of an elevator which leads to a short tunnel and then a 305-metre boardwalk beside the foaming waters with observation points along the way. Access is 40 metres north of the Whirlpool Rapids Bridge opposite the Ramada Inn on River Road.

Merritt Trail

This 11-kilometre urban trail gives visitors the best places to encounter the ruins of the second Welland Canal. Much of the trail follows the valley of Twelve Mile Creek, which was the course followed by the first two versions of the canal. The trail begins (or ends) at Bradley Street in south St. Catharines where the lock ruins of the second Welland Canal are visible in Mountain Locks Park. As the name implies, those locks form a step feature as the canal mounted the steep climb up the escarpment and earned it the nickname Neptune's Staircase. In this park, the trail lies along the towpaths where horses or oxen dragged the schooners or barges through the more than 40 locks that were required to surmount the escarpment and complete the journey to Lake Erie.

From the park, the trail continues through St. Catharines to Martindale Road. It is not a continuous nature trail; many sections are intermittent and follow St. Catharines' streets. Otherwise, it is a stone dust trail which allows history buffs close-up views of some of the Welland Canal's oldest locks.

At Port Dalhousie, the Lock 1 station of the Second and Third Canals are preserved. The route of the Third Canal through St. Catharines and Thorold was much straighter and portions of it lie beneath the built-up area of Thorold. The mountain locks of the third canal lie on the east side of Lock 7 of the current canal and are not publicly accessible.

Twenty Valley Trail

This short trail is not 20 miles long, but rather follows the valley of Twenty Mile Creek from the Lincoln Museum in Jordan

Village to the Ball's Falls Conservation Area. Many of the creeks which flow into the western end of Lake Ontario include the word "mile," such as Twenty Mile Creek. That nomenclature dates from sailing days when the mouths of the various creeks and rivers were named for their distance from the mouth of the Niagara River, an important shipping point.

As the trail follows the valley, it can be steep and uneven, and occasionally difficult to follow. It winds through dense forest and passes caves hidden in the limestone canyon walls. The trail continues up the valley and ends at the double cascades in the Ball's Falls Conservation Area. The trail links with the Bruce Trail in the Ball's Falls Conservation Area with its ghost town and a double waterfall. The lower falls tumble over a sheer cliff beside the old mill, which is now a museum.

Among other points of interest along the Twenty Valley Creek is the village of Jordan Station. A conscientious heritage-loving owner has authentically preserved the 1890s Grand Trunk Railway station which is now their private home. It sits on Prince William Street close to its original site. Jordan Station dates from 1853 when the Great Western Railway laid its tracks through the Niagara Peninsula.

The popular tourist village of Jordan lies just two kilometres south from the station village and contains a string of shops and the Cave Spring Vineyard, where wine tastings are available.

These rocks on a trail in the Niagara Glen show the result of limestone erosion caused by melt waters from ancient glaciers.

Church Street is a short side street which leads from Main Street to the new Lincoln Museum and Cultural Centre. The site includes a small pioneer village with the village's former one-room school and Niagara's oldest Mennonite meeting house. Trail hikers can start here by descending a staircase into the valley.

Trails of Short Hills Provincial Park

This free park is renowned for its Carolinian forest and its geology. It is so named due to the erosion of the glacial deposits from 20,000 years ago which moulded the land into a jumble of small but steep hills and valleys. Seven trails include a portion of the Bruce Trail, which was twinned with the Rim of Africa Trail and is called the Rim of Africa Friendship Trail. (The Rim of Africa is a mountain passage in the Cape Fold Mountains in South Africa.)

The trail system offers visitors the chance to stroll through the hills and forests and visit the seasonal Swayze Falls, the largest of several small waterfalls which often run dry during the late summer. Four of the seven trails are all-purpose trails for hiking, biking and horseback riding. Access points are Regional Road 81 (Pelham Road) and Roland Road.

Short Hills Provincial Park covers an area of 660 hectares, making it the largest provincial park in the Niagara region.

Gord Harry Trail

This is a 13-kilometre trail which follows the former Grand Trunk Railway roadbed between Quarry Road and Station Road west of Port Colborne. It shares parking space and access with the Wainfleet Wetlands Conservation Area. It is noted for its bird-watching opportunities and small mammals. It also offers access to the quarry lake within the conservation area. Gord Harry was a noted local conservationist.

Stone stairs highlight the challenges of the trails in Niagara Glen.

DAY TRIPS AND EXPLORATIONS — WATER AND RAIL

BRIDGING THE GAP

Niagara River Bridges

Among the most dramatic of Niagara's engineering achievements are the massive and historic bridges which stretch across the swirling waters and mighty chasm of the Niagara River. Today, there are a half-dozen bridges: the Queenston-Lewiston Bridge, the Lower Steel Arch Bridge (also called the Whirlpool Rapids Bridge), the abandoned Michigan Central Railway Bridge, the Rainbow Bridge, the International Railway Bridge, and the busy Peace Bridge.

    The first attempt to construct a permanent link over the gorge was the Niagara Falls Suspension Bridge, across the narrowest part of the gorge downstream from the falls. But how to begin the work when the tortuous rapids and a deep abyss lay between the two sides of the river?

    Eventually the builders came up with the idea of flying a kite over the gorge from the Canadian side (to take advantage of prevailing winds), with a string along which a cable could be later attached. Finally, on August 1, 1848, the suspension bridge opened to traffic. That must have been a harrowing experience, as the bridge consisted

The Peace Bridge spans the Niagara River between Fort Erie, Ontario and Buffalo, New York.

Previous spread: **The Rainbow Bridge.**

Trucks line up to cross the Queenston-Lewiston Bridge to enter the United States.

of little more than a series of planks suspended between the cables. A similar idea was tried between Lewiston and Queenston beneath the great gates of the escarpment, and was completed in 1850.

Suspension bridges, however, are susceptible to gale-force winds which cause them to buckle and twist and then collapse in a twisted heap of wood and metal; that was the fate of the first Queenston to Lewiston bridge in 1854. It had lasted a mere four years.

In 1899, the Falls View Suspension Bridge in Niagara Falls was dismantled and rebuilt across the river at Queenston. It carried not just horse-drawn vehicles, but also the trolleys of the Niagara Falls Parks and River scenic tour train as well. In 1962, long after the rails had been lifted, the bridge came down in a twisted heap during a fierce gale. Only a few stone abutments remain on the riverbank where York Road in Queenston ended. The last portion of the road is now a trail of deteriorating asphalt that ends at the river.

The arrival of the railways in 1853 ushered in the need for a bridge capable of supporting the heavy weight of steam engines and the cars which they pulled. In 1855, a bridge engineer named John Roebling, who later gained fame for his design for the Brooklyn Bridge, conceived of a fixed truss suspension bridge over the gorge downstream from the falls. It had an added feature of allowing not only trains but, by building a lower level on the bridge, pedestrians and wagons to cross as well.

By 1877, however, trains were getting heavier and a new and sturdier bridge was needed. By this time, improved engineering had developed the cantilever steel arch bridge. These bridges were supported from below, rather than suspended from above, and such was the next new railway bridge. Completed in 1897, the new steel arch bridge also had two layers, the upper deck for trains and the lower deck for vehicular traffic.

This structure still stands and is one of Niagara's most historic bridges. Known now as the Whirlpool Rapids Bridge, the vehicle entrance and office are on River Road at Bridge Street in Niagara Falls while the trains rumble overhead. The result of the decline in the use of the bridge by rail traffic and passenger cars can be seen in the vacant tourist shops, restaurants, and hotels which line the nearby streets. The bridge is for NEXUS pass holders only.

Michigan Central Railway Bridge

Adjacent to it, and formerly merging with it on the American side, is the Michigan Central Railway Bridge, also a steel arch structure. Construction began in 1924, and the bridge opened in 1925. This bridge replaced the Niagara Cantilever Bridge that crossed in the same area from 1883 to 1925. Although rail traffic no longer uses the bridge, it remains an important part of Niagara's railway legacy.

Queenston-Lewiston Bridge

Since 1962, the new high-level four-lane Queenston-Lewiston Bridge carries cross-border traffic more than 120 metres above the river from Ontario's Highway 405 to Interstate 190 on the American side. Built using a single steel arch, the bridge stretches 260 metres from cliff to cliff and is the fourth-busiest international crossing in Canada. Wait times can last up to two hours. For anyone not crossing, the best view of the imposing structure is from the viewing area on the Parkway, a short distance south of the Sir Adam Beck Generating Station.

Rainbow Bridge

Shortly after the loss of the Honeymoon Bridge, the Niagara Falls Bridge Commission launched plans for a new steel arch replacement bridge which they named the Rainbow Bridge. In 1939, King George VI and Queen Elizabeth visited Niagara Falls and, on June 7, dedicated the site of the future Rainbow Bridge on the Canadian shore with a monument commemorating the occasion.

On May 4, 1940, construction on the new Rainbow Bridge began. The span of the current bridge is 440 metres and it arches 202 metres above the surface of the water. The Rainbow Bridge Plaza opened in 1941. This elaborate entranceway was decorated with panels of bas relief stone carvings by noted Canadian artists Florence Wyle and Frances Loring. The expansion of the Canadian entrance, carried out in 1997, meant that six of these panels needed to be relocated and are now on view along the adjacent riverside pedestrian walk under the bridge.

The most striking feature of the bridge is the 50-metre-high carillon tower with 55 tuned bells inside. The tower appeared in the 1953 Marilyn Monroe movie *Niagara*. Unfortunately, as the tower is now within the customs compound it is not accessible to the public, but is sufficiently high that it can be viewed from a distance.

Mather's Bridge of Peace

At the south end of the river rises the iconic Peace Bridge. In 1919, the bridge design was approved and in June 1927 the Peace Bridge opened with the ceremonies taking place two months later. In attendance were the Prince of Wales (Edward VIII), his brother Prince George (George VI), Prime Minister Mackenzie King, and his British counterpart, Stanley Baldwin. Also present were the Ontario Premier, the United States Vice President and Secretary of State, and the Governor of New York State.

The five arched spans extend 1.77 kilometres across the river and took two years to complete. In 1940, the Niagara Parks Commission dedicated a monument to Alonzo Mather, an early advocate for a bridge at this location, which stands at the Fort Erie entrance to the bridge and offers the best views of the bridge itself. Today, more than one million trucks cross each year and can experience waits of up to four hours.

A short distance downstream, the International Railway Bridge opened in 1873, giving American railways a convenient shortcut to markets in Michigan. It remains in use.

A view of the tracks across the International Railway Bridge in Fort Erie.

ENGINEERING MARVEL
The Welland Canal

In 1825, the Erie Canal opened across New York State, providing a vital direct link between the Great Lakes and the Atlantic Ocean ports, with 82 locks to navigate between Albany and Buffalo.

It was with the construction of the Erie Canal that mill owner William Hamilton Merritt realized the need for an all-Canadian route from the upper lakes to the Montreal seaports. Along with other merchants, he lobbied for a canal to link Lake Erie and Lake Ontario. The valley of Twelve Mile Creek was selected as the ideal route for the canal. Due to the need to surmount the mighty ramparts of the Niagara Escarpment, it would prove to be one of North America's most challenging feats of canal building.

Construction began in Allanburg in 1824, and by 1829 the canal opened for shipping to Chippawa on the Niagara River by way of Port Robinson and the Welland River. By 1833, the "big dig" had extended the canal directly southward from Port Robinson to Port Colborne on Lake Erie. But the deterioration of the first wooden locks and the increasing size of the ships using them meant that an upgrade was needed. In 1845 new larger masonry locks were put in place, allowing passage for the larger vessels.

An aerial view of the Twin Flight Locks engineering marvel at Thorold.

The *Whitefish Bay* lake freighter squeezes into Lock 3, traveling north on the Welland Canal.

The third Welland Canal took a more direct path from Port Dalhousie to Allanburg, leaving behind the Twelve Mile Creek route. From Allanburg the canal continued to follow the previous path to Port Colborne. Construction on the third canal was completed in 1887.

With more shipping, even the third canal proved inadequate, and in 1913 work on a fourth canal began. Interrupted by World War I, work did not finish until 1932. An entirely new route was chosen. The entry from Lake Ontario was moved east to Port Weller, and the number of locks reduced to seven, plus an eighth control lock at Port Colborne. Today, this canal remains in use. Portions of both the second and third canals continued to function until 1935. With the completion of the fourth canal, they became redundant. Most of the third canal was buried beneath the growing cities of St. Catharines and Thorold.

Then, in 1972, a bypass which carried the canal around the streets of Welland opened. It was larger still and removed the obstacle of the vehicular lift bridge on Welland's main street.

Today, massive vessels, both lake and ocean freighters, take only 11 hours to complete the 43.5 kilometres from end to end. To mount the escarpment, the canal now rises over 100 metres over a distance of 11 kilometres from Lock 1 to Lock 7 at the crest of the escarpment. The world-famous twin flight locks, 4, 5 and 6 at Thorold, lift the vessels 42.5 metres through three twinned step locks to surmount the face of the Niagara Escarpment. Lock 7 marks the crest of the ridge.

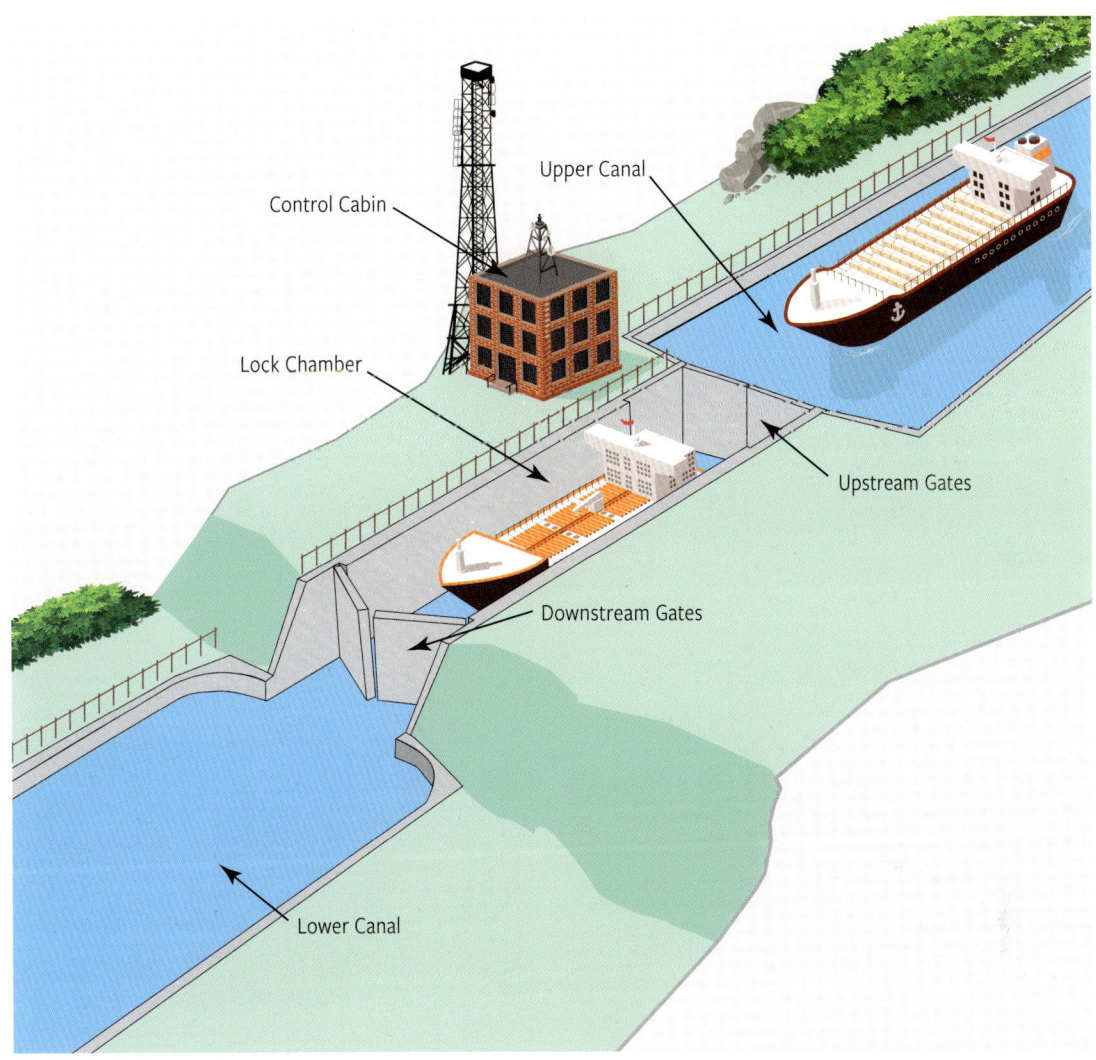

This illustration shows how the Welland Canal raises and lowers ships in a series of seven locks up and down the Niagara Escarpment.

Each year more than 3,000 passages take place with the ships carrying more than 30 million tonnes of grain, iron ore, coal, salt and steel. A record 66 million tonnes passed through the canal in 1974.

Visiting the Locks

The entrance for the first three canals remained at Port Dalhousie and here early canal features have survived. Two historic lighthouses, known as range lighthouses, one at the outer entrance, the other further in, still guide today's recreational boats into the large harbour and marina.

In 1898, the inner lighthouse was destroyed by lightning and replaced with the structure which stands today. Now

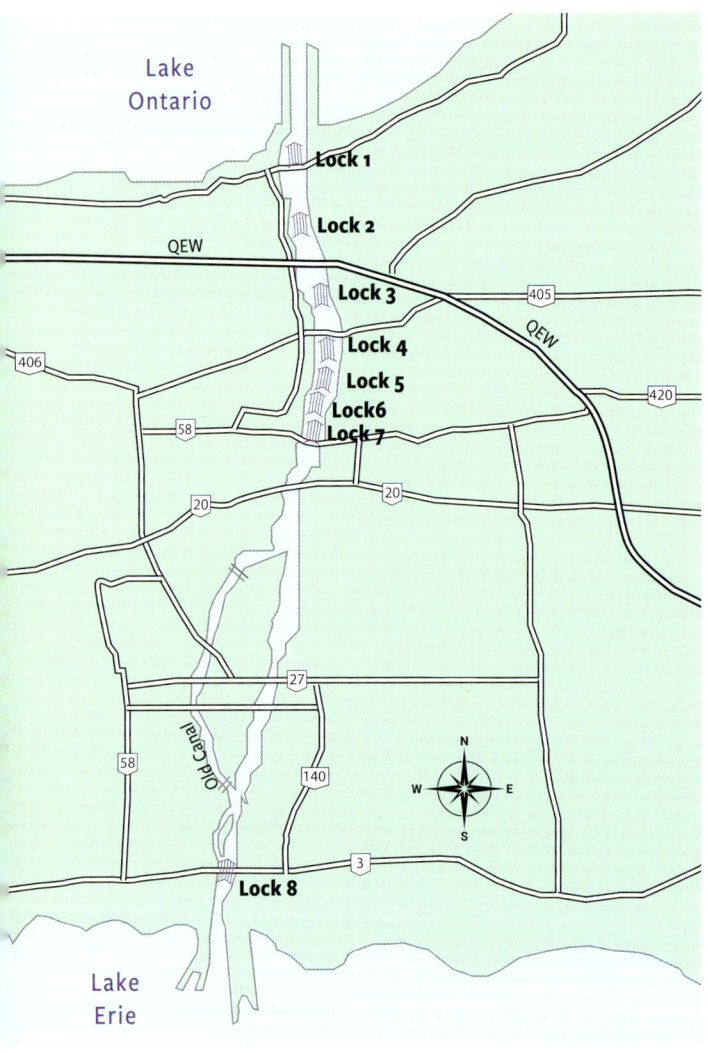

This illustration shows the location of the eight locks that make up the Welland Canal.

decommissioned, the inner lighthouse was designated a Recognized Federal Heritage Building in 1990. In 1997 it was transferred to the City of St. Catharines. The lighthouse was restored between 2000 and 2002. The outer 1878 lighthouse remains active today.

Welland provides several reminders of the canal's legacy and history. Bridge 13, a looming vertical lift bridge, decommissioned when the canal bypass opened in 1972, is a Welland landmark connecting Main Street East and West over the waterway.

North of Main Street on Boardwalk Street, sit remains of the second canal's aqueduct, constructed in 1840 to permit the second canal to pass over the Welland River. Merritt Park, which runs along the canal-bank south from Main Street, contains the Welland Canal Fallen Workers Memorial, dedicated to the 137 men who were killed building the Welland Canal.

The intersection of Prince Charles Drive and Ontario (Broadway) Road in Welland exposes a portion of the old lock from the 1845 feeder canal. Although the feeder canal is buried at this point, the site offers historical information on this important component of the early days of the canal. Built to add a source of water from the Grand River to the main canal, the feeder canal also allowed for barges to navigate between the Grand River and the main canal. It remains visible as a weedy ditch from Welland to Port Maitland on the Grand River, where the remains of a stone lock still survive. The location of the historic plaque in Welland is on Federal Road east of Prince Charles Road.

From Main Street in Welland, landscaped walkways continue south along the banks of the canal as does Canal Bank Road. Canal Terrace, between King and Division Streets is lined with benches, gardens and a number of panels describing the history of the canal, a perfect complement to the many murals along Main and King Streets. The Welland Museum on King Street can fill in the gaps regarding the area's industrial development.

The elegant lighthouse at Point Abino in Fort Erie is not accessible to the public.

Port Robinson, although off today's beaten path, was the original terminus of the first canal and contains the preserved remains of the lock structure which fed the waters on the canal into the Welland River.

Located in Gravelly Bay in Port Colborne, two lighthouses guided ships into the Welland Canal. The inner lighthouse, built in 1902, was visible from five kilometres away. The outer lighthouse, added in 1928, once boasted the loudest foghorn on the Canadian side of the Great Lakes. While both have been decommissioned, tours are held during Port Colborne's Canal Days Festival by the Friends of the Port Colborne Lighthouses.

One of the two historic lighthouses that guard the harbour entrance to Port Dalhousie.

The historic Robin Hood silos still dominate the view from the Welland Canal near Port Colborne.

Point Abino lighthouse is the most stunning lighthouse on the Ontario side of the Great Lakes. While not directly on the Welland Canal, it served to guide vessels along the tricky shoreline of Lake Erie to the Port Colborne harbour. It was constructed in 1917 following the destruction of an earlier light ship. Designed in the late neoclassical style, the lighthouse consists of a square, slightly tapered column rising from one end of a rectangular, flat-roofed, single-storey base.

The Lighthouse was decommissioned in 1996 and in 1998 became a National Historic Site of Canada. The structure is recognized for its unusual shape, classical detailing, and efficiency of structural design. It is considered as one of the most aesthetically stunning concrete lighthouses in Canada. The Lighthouse consists of three structures: the deck, tower and fog alarm building. The former keeper's dwelling survives nearby. The lighthouse is now a National Historic Site of Canada. As this fine old lighthouse is only accessible along a private gated road, visitors must arrange tours through the Town of Fort Erie.

THE WELLAND CANAL PARKWAY

The Welland Canal Parkway Trail allows cyclists and motorists an opportunity to follow today's operating canal from Lock 1 through to Lock 7 at the top of the escarpment.

The Parkway Trail commences beside Lock 1 on Lakeshore Road in Port Weller, the entry from Lake Ontario for the 4th Welland Canal. Here a large bascule bridge rises to allow the ships to pass.

A side trail on the west side of the canal leads north from the Lakeshore Road to the historic lighthouse on Lake Ontario. Most of the trail is limited to cyclists and hikers. On the east side of the bridge, Broadway Avenue leads north from Lakeshore and comes to a fork where Seaway Haulage Road to the left leads to a viewing area on the side of the Canal.

Bunting Road, the start of the Welland Canal Parkway Trail, makes its way south from Lakeshore Road and leads to Charles Ansell Park where views of the ships passing under the Port Weller bridge are available. On the opposite side of the canal the Heddle Shipyards may have a ship in for refurbishing. Both the cycle path and the road continue south on Bunting Road to a fork to the left onto the marked Welland Canal Parkway Trail and to Lock 2.

After passing Lock 2, the Parkway Trail passes beneath the soaring Garden City Skyway and on to the canal's main viewing point, the Lock 3 St. Catharines Museum and Welland Canals Centre both housed in the same structure. A three-level viewing platform beside the lock gives visitors an up-close view of the massive ships easing into the narrow space between hull and wall. The process of lowering and raising the ships takes about 12 minutes.

A small gift shop inside the centre offers books, snacks and coffee, while the times of the next ships are posted nearby. An elevator rises to the third level which exits to the platform for those not wishing to climb the platform stairs.

The St. Catharines Museum, also within the centre, is open to visitors and contains a walk-through display depicting the early days of the city and the canal.

From Lock 3, the Parkway Trail continues across Glendale Avenue with one of the Canal's iconic steel lift bridges. This brings the route to one of the canal's engineering marvels, the twin flight lift locks, Locks 4, 5 and 6. With flight locks, the waters flow from one lock directly into the lock below. Being twinned, the locks permit ships to lock through simultaneously in both directions. At the top of the climb is the Lock 7 viewing platform and snack bar and a popular tourist photo destination, the Kissing Rock.

Here the vehicular route detours along the streets of Thorold, away from the canal while the cycle route continues along the canal.

Opportunities to view the canal resume at Allanburg where another historic lift bridge crosses the waterway. Beside it an historical stone cairn celebrates the ground-breaking of the first canal at this location.

In Port Colborne, the old and the new canals finally rejoin beside the Clarence Street vertical lift bridge. Here, Lock 8 regulates the flow between Lake Erie and the waters of the canal offering another opportunity for a park-side view of the vessels inching their way into the lock.

Two canal related industries in Port Colborne include the grain elevators at the Lake Erie harbour and, north of Lock 8, the historic Robin Hood Flour Mill silos.

On the canal-side main street of Port Colborne, West Street, ship watchers can enjoy a coffee while viewing the ships that pass in the night (and day).

The entrance to the St. Catharines Museum and Lock 3 viewing platform.

RIDING THE RAILS
Niagara's Railway Legacy

Once, Niagara was crisscrossed with a busy spider's web of railway lines. Although Niagara's rail days are mostly long gone, there still remains much for die-hard rail enthusiasts to see.

Ontario's First Railway

The first railway to operate in the region was built to carry people and products around the falls. Following the route of an earlier Indigenous portage, the railway ran between Chippawa, at the confluence of the Niagara and the Welland rivers, and Queenston at the outlet of the Niagara Gorge. The route of that portage eventually became today's Portage Road.

In 1825, ground was broken at Allanburg for the first Welland Canal. The canal opened in 1829 but passage was slow, requiring 11 days to complete and 40 locks to navigate. And it was obviously seasonal.

To allow businesses along the Portage Road to compete with the new canal, a portage railway was begun. This was known as the Erie and Ontario Railway. Work began in 1835 and was completed

A VIA Rail/Amtrak passenger train en route from Toronto to New York City pauses at the historic Niagara Falls station to embark passengers.

in 1845. The railcars were drawn by teams of four horses. The rails were wood and topped with iron strips. Each car could carry twenty passengers, their baggage perched precariously on the roof.

In 1852, steam locomotives replaced the struggling teams of horses, and the route was moved closer to the then villages of Clifton and Elgin. It was subsequently realigned again and extended to Niagara-on-the-Lake (then simply called Niagara), and a decade later reached Fort Erie, when it was renamed the Erie and Niagara Railway. In 1869, it came under the ownership of the larger Canada Southern Railway (CSR).

The CSR began running three trains a day from the ferry dock at Fort Erie, where the Buffalo ferries arrived, to Niagara-on-the-Lake to meet the ferry service from Toronto and Hamilton. In effect it was a portage between the two lakes.

Over the following decades ownership underwent a series of changes. The Erie and Niagara portion of the line between Clifton and Niagara-on-the-Lake ended passenger service in the 1920s and stopped running trains altogether in 1959.

The legacy of this early line has left rail lovers little to see. The stations there were demolished or relocated and most of the right of way was absorbed into the road system. However, the former railway station on King Street in Niagara-on-the-Lake,

Known historically as Bridge # 17, this historic railway lift bridge crosses an abandoned portion of the Welland Canal near Dain City.

The historic Niagara-on-the-Lake downtown train station is now a busy gift shop.

is now a gift shop in the heart of the busy tourist town. A pair of historic hotels stand on Melville Street including the Harbour House and the King George III Inn.

Upper Canada Heritage Trail

Between St David's and Niagara-on-the-Lake, however, the former right-of-way became the Upper Canada Heritage Trail. Opened in 1985, the trail's northern terminal lies at the southwest corner of King and John Streets in Niagara-on-the-Lake. From there, it angles southward through the town's suburbs before crossing farm fields to parallel Concession 1 Road. It remains a well-maintained path as far as East West Line. Beyond that it is scarcely visible and is called a greenway, not a trail.

In Niagara Falls, at the corner of Stanley Avenue and Morrison Street near the entrance to Oakes Park Stadium, a stone cairn erected in 1931 commemorates the Erie and Ontario Railway as the first railroad in Upper Canada.

Meanwhile, south and west of Niagara Falls, the CPR, the latest operator of the line, included a link from Crowland Junction at the south end of Welland, to its rail yard at Montrose at the south end of Niagara Falls. In 1905 tracks ran diagonally through the city to the Michigan Central Railroad steel arch bridge over the Niagara River beside the older Grand Trunk Railway steel arch bridge. While the old Grand

Trunk bridge still sees CN and Amtrak trains crossing it, the Michigan Central bridge sits abandoned. Both structures are visible from River Road at the north end of the city.

Tracks from the CPR's lines further west still remain in place for a short distance beyond the former divisional yards at Montrose to serve local industry in the southern portion of Niagara Falls and to provide storage tracks for the railway's maintenance-of-way vehicles.

The only surviving building in Niagara Falls with a relationship to this railway is the large stone 19th century customs house at Park and Zimmerman. Originally known as the Dominion Public Building, it was designed by government architect Thomas Fuller (who designed the first parliament buildings in Ottawa) and was constructed at a cost of $30,000. It served as post office (1885-1930), customs house (1885-1952) and a police station (1952-1976). Although boarded up, it occasionally resurfaces as a film location.

Great Gorge Railway

Perhaps the most spectacular of the Niagara rail routes was the Niagara Parks and River Railway. Known as the Great Gorge Route, it took tourists along the awe-inspiring brink of the Niagara Gorge.

After the rail line opened in 1893, so many tourists were flocking to ride it that the railway doubled its tracks. Meanwhile, on the American side, a comparable rail line opened along the base of the gorge allowing riders a close-up view of the turbulent rapids and the whirlpool.

With the completion of two important bridges, the Queenston-Lewiston Suspension Bridge and the Rainbow Bridge in Niagara Falls, the two lines joined their routes in 1902, and established the Great Gorge Route. The line operated 38 trolley cars, most of them open-sided with bench seats that spanned the width of the narrow vehicles.

Sadly, fatal accidents became a problem, notably on the American side. In 1915, a trolley leapt the tracks killing 13 people, and two years later another toppled into the whirlpool rapids drowning a dozen people.

In 1932, the Niagara Parks Commission purchased the Canadian portion of the line and removed the tracks. The American operation continued for a few more years until more rockslides brought that portion to an end. Along the Canadian route, only a portion of a filled-in trestle remains visible opposite the golf course. A plaque commemorates this once busy tour train.

There remain a few other components of the line for history buffs to see. The busy Table Rock House formerly served as a station for the railway, although that early station is now only a portion of the expanded current structure. But two other lesser-known stations survive. The Niagara Glen Nature Centre bears the architectural hallmarks of a typical railway station of the Niagara Falls Park and River Railway, while one of the buildings in the botanical gardens although relocated from its original location along the line, is also a one-time station building and is used now by garden staff.

Great Western Railway

In addition to these pioneering rail lines, Niagara was crisscrossed by five major railway lines. The Great Western Railway was the first rail line to cross southern Ontario. The line was essentially a shortcut for American rail traffic moving from New York to the American cities beyond Windsor and Sarnia where the line crossed back into the United States. It remains to this day a busy CN line.

Along the line the GWR left behind a legacy of elegant stations, most of them designed by renowned station architect Joseph Hobson. Fine examples of his work still grace the tracks at Brantford, Woodstock, Ingersoll, and Chatham. His station in Niagara Falls, then called Clifton, is a large gothic brick station used today by VIA Rail, GO Transit, and Amtrak. Opposite the station stand early hotels which once served the train passengers, now vacant and boarded up.

Jordan Station village contains the sole surviving station of the GTR era, now relocated to the south side of Prince William Street in the village. Happily, the heritage conscious owners have authentically restored its original paint scheme and other external features.

The Port Robinson station is now part of CN's busy Niagara switching yards.

Canada Southern Railway

Like the GWR, the Canada Southern was yet another shortcut to link American industrial centres in New York State with Michigan. The line crossed the Niagara River at Fort Erie on the International Railway Bridge and angled across the countryside to the sleepy Sarnia suburb of Corunna. Originally conceived as the Niagara and Detroit Rivers Railroad in the 1840s, trains did not start passing along the tracks until 1873 when the International Railway Bridge over the Niagara River at Fort Erie was opened.

Toronto, Hamilton and Buffalo Railway

Although the charter which it received in 1884 mandated that this small railway run between Toronto and Buffalo via the International Bridge at Fort Erie, the railroad did not make it to either city. Its operations began in 1892 by taking over two smaller lines that originated in Brantford, and by 1895 completed a link between Hamilton and Welland. There it connected with the Canada Southern Railway to justify its connection to Buffalo, while to reach

Toronto it acquired running rights over the Grand Trunk Railway. To reach Welland, however, it needed to construct a steep section up the escarpment near Grimsby. In addition, two short branch lines connected it to Port Colborne and Dunnville.

The CPR and the New York Central Railroad bought the TH&B in 1895 and the CPR took 90 percent ownership in 1977. With the construction of the Welland Canal bypass in 1972, the railway lines were rerouted to run beneath the canal. Further north, the current CN tracks cross the canal on a lift bridge at Thorold. Train movements through the tunnel are visible from Townline Tunnel Road 58A, while those crossing the Thorold bridge may be witnessed from the Lock 7 Viewing Platform.

Buffalo, Brantford and Goderich Railway

Another effort to link American markets in New York with the Great Lakes grain shipments, the BB&G opened between Fort Erie and Goderich in 1858. The line ran to the Grand River where it angled north to Dunnville, and then on to Brantford, Paris, Stratford until it reached its terminal at Goderich.

The line facilitated American access to the beaches of Lake Erie. Communities such as Crystal Beach, Sherkston and Lowbanks boomed with American tourists. These early summer resorts are now mostly relegated to the history books. However, there remains some evidence of that early prosperity in Port Colborne.

Situated on the Lake Erie shore adjacent to the residential part of the town, a community of wealthy American families from the American South created a private colony named Solid Comfort, with a small railway station on the BB&G for their exclusive use. Until the 1930s, the residents would trade the heat of the southern summers for the breezes of the lake. In the 1930s, due to the Great Depression and overdue taxes, the colony disbanded.

Nevertheless, a few of the colony's heritage features remain. The stone gates which once kept unwanted Canadians away from their beaches, still guard the entrance to Tennessee Avenue where a grand building known as the Casino (a dance hall) still stands. These gates are now a designated heritage feature. Amid the newer homes, there also remain a few of the earlier southern style homes from those heady days.

Port Colborne also boasts the only surviving station along the route, a CN station erected in 1927, now repurposed as a restaurant. It stands beside the one-time locks of the second Welland Canal.

Friendship Rail-Trail

This is a trail that follows the abandoned roadbed of the Buffalo, Brantford and Goderich Railroad (BB&G). Opened in 1854, the railway was abandoned between Fort Erie and Caledonia in 1985 and the portion between Fort Erie and Port Colborne became the Friendship Trail. This 16-kilometre trail is straight and flat, and paved for much of the way.

Lying inland from Lake Erie's shore, it offers little in the way of shoreline scenery, although it does traverse pleasant farmland. The trail begins at Port Colborne

Years of diligent volunteer labour have brought to life Niagara's railway museum in Fort Erie.

Seaway Park on Fraser Street where it crossed the two canals by means of a vertical lift and a swing bridge. In Fort Erie the eastern end point lies on Edgemere Road east of Kraft Road. While the railway lift bridge over the fourth canal in Port Colborne has been removed, remains of the former railway swing bridge over the older canal still remain beside the vehicular lift bridge.

Following the west side of the canal, the newer route of the rail line swings in front of the former station and then branches south to the grain elevator on the lake. Here it operates as the Trillium Railway, formerly the Port Colborne Harbour Railway.

The rail trail resumes west of Port Colborne as the Gord Harry Trail.

Welland Railway

In 1853, pressure was building for a north-south route between Port Dalhousie on Lake Ontario and Port Colborne on Lake Erie. Because of disagreements between municipal governments in St. Catharines and Niagara Falls, the Welland Railway's opening did not occur until 1861.

Since 1917, the CN Railway, which absorbed many of Ontario's rail lines, has removed much of the Welland Railway's historic infrastructure. One part of the legacy that remains is the active rail yards in Port Robinson north of Canby, now part of the Trillium Railway.

The Trillium Railway is Niagara Region's latest railroad, the first since CP came into Niagara. Trillium established the Port Colborne Harbour Railway in 1997. Grain cars line the tracks at Port Colborne's grain elevator on Lake Erie.

Heritage Legacy Stations

As a once-important railway hub, Niagara contained the usual rail features, including roundhouses, water towers, accommodations for train crews, rail yards, and more than two dozen stations.

Disregarding the heritage value of their stations, both CN Rail and CP Rail began demolishing these heritage buildings once the railways had no further use for them. Despite the hurdles which the railways placed before those who tried to save these structures, a few old stations still survive.

Documented surviving stations in Niagara Region include Allanburg (now a private residence), Bridgeburg and Ridgeway (both on display at the Fort Erie Railway Museum), Grimsby (the community's original 1853 GWR station near original site), Jordan (on Prince William Road, near its original site), Niagara Falls (active station serving VIA, GO Transit and Amtrak on Bridge Street), Niagara-on-the-Lake (now a gift shop on its original site on King Street) and Port Colborne (on its original site on West Street in downtown Port Colborne now containing offices and a restaurant).

Lost in the bushes of the Wainfleet peat bog lie the vanishing remains of the Erie Peat Railway. From 1940 to the mid 1980s the Erie Peat Company operated a small two-foot gauge railway to haul peat from the bog to their nearby processing plant. Following a fire in the bog in 1983, the railway was abandoned, and peat extraction ceased. A portion of the bog was acquired by the government and is now the Wainfleet Bog Conservation Area.

The locomotives and rolling stock were later removed by local railway enthusiasts. The rails, approximately five kilometres in length, can still be seen and form part of the trail system through the bog which is now a nature conservation area.

Niagara Railway Museum

Housed in the former Canadian National Railway diesel shop in Fort Erie, the Niagara Railway Museum houses railway equipment, documents, photographs and a model railway.

The founders of the museum began actively assembling the collection in 1994. In 1996, the museum added a CP rail track motorcar, and a pair of baggage cars. By 2001, the collection had grown to include three box cars and a stone track grinder. There are also railway documents, manuals and 300 blueprints. In 2006, the NRM acquired the last remaining steam locomotive from the Sir Adam Beck Generating Station, HEPC #46, built in 1920. Today it is a prime focus of the NRM's display. Donations included a track mobile, and a 40-ton diesel engine. The oldest of the boxcars is a 1939 TH&B boxcar.

To find a place to display this growing collection proved a challenge. Finally in 2010, after years of searching, the NRM moved into the 1950s-era CNR diesel shop which had been closed since 1989. Visitors to the site, which is only open on select dates, can enjoy a short ride on a 1948 25-ton diesel. As an added treat, rail traffic may rumble past on its way to or from the International Bridge. The Museum is located at the end of Warren Street west of Lewis Street in Fort Erie.

Fort Erie Railway Museum

A short drive from the Niagara Railway Museum leads to yet another railway museum, the Fort Erie Railway Museum. Open to the public daily, the outdoor static displays include a steam locomotive, a caboose and a pair of railway stations. Dominating the site is CNR's massive 4-8-4 steam locomotive which was built in 1942 and continued in service until well into the 1960s.

Flanking the steam engine are the former Ridgeway Grand Trunk train station, with its hip roof gables and a square tower above the agent's bay, as well as a porte-cochere on the end of the gleaming white structure. The second station was used to monitor traffic over the International Bridge and now contains the ticket counter for entry into the Ridgeway station building and gift shop.

All Aboard!

Despite the many legacies of Niagara's rail days, there remain few opportunities to actually ride in a train. In fact, the only remaining active passenger rail lines are GO Transit from Toronto and Hamilton to the Niagara Falls station and VIA Rail's daily Maple Leaf train. GO Transit offers special summer weekend bike trains as well as weekday commuter service. GO Transit's bike trains run three times a day on Saturdays, Sundays and holidays until Canadian Thanksgiving and include three special coaches, each with a capacity of 18 bikes. Passengers need only walk a few paces to board waiting WEGO buses run by Niagara Parks to the many attractions in the vicinity. In addition, Amtrak partners with VIA Rail to operate a daily run between Toronto and New York City, known as the Maple Leaf which stops at Niagara Falls.

WEGO buses carry passengers to all the important attractions in the area.

INDEX

Act to Limit Slavery, 1793, 35, 39
Adam Beck Generating Station, 144, 232
A La Gallarie Bed and Breakfast, 156
American Falls, 20
Appleton Boys School, 157
Art Gallery, 104–107
    Gate Street Studio, 107
    Jordan, 107
    King Street, 107
    Niagara Falls, 104
    Niagara Image, 106–107
    Northern Expressions Inuit, 105, 107

Baldwin, Stanley, 212
Ball, George, 163–164
Ball, John, 163–164
Ball's Falls, 103, 163–165, 167, 179, 196–197, 203
Bampfield Hall, 157
Bampfield, James, 157
Barnett, Thomas, 44, 87
Battle of
    Beaver Dams, 128, 135
    Chippawa, 138
    Cooks Mills, 137
    Frenchman's Creek, 137
    Lundy's Lane, 135–137, 174
    Queenston Heights, 128
    Ridgeway, 80, 138
Benson, James, 153
Bertie Street ferry landing, 36

Bethel Chapel, 77
Black Heritage, Niagara's, 35–39
Blue Ghost Tunnel *see* Merritton Tunnel
Borden's Dairy, 59
Brant, John, 32, 132
Brant, Joseph, 30
Bridge,
    Falls View Suspension, 68, 209–210
    Garden City Skyway, 150
    International Railway, 212–213, 228, 233
    Michigan Central Railway, 45, 209, 211
    Niagara Cantilever, 45
    Peace, 150, 208–209, 212
    Queenston-Lewiston, 68, 209–211
    Rainbow International, 47, 209, 211–212
    Whirlpool Rapids, 45, 209, 211
Bright, John, 157
Bright, Thomas, 160
Bright's Wines, 156
Brock's Cenotaph, 136
Brock's Monument, 130–131, 136, 144
Brock University, 111, 154, 192
Brock, General Sir Isaac, 128, 130–131, 173
Brockamour Manor, 173
Brown Homestead, 30, 160–161
Brown, John, 160–161

Bruce Trail Conservancy, 196, 198
Burton, Pierre, 89
Butler, John, 133–134
Butler's Rangers, 117–118

Cairns, Fred, 58
Canada's Got Talent, 95
Canby, Benjamin, 165
Cardinal, Douglas, 32
Carr-Millar-McMillan Block, 77
Carpet Bag Theatre troupe, 104
Carter, Lewis, 159
Casino Niagara, 48, 87, 91
Casino Tower *see* Oneida Tower
Chandler, Samuel, 165
Chautauqua Movement, the, 169–172
Church,
    Beaver Dams Methodist, 166
    British Methodist Episcopal, 36
    Holy Trinity, 148
    St. John's Anglican, 148
    St. Mark's, 39
Churchill, Winston, 142
Claydon, Jeff, 136
Clifton Hill, 48, 55, 86, 89–90
Clock Tower, Memorial, 67
"Coloured Cemetery," 37
"Coloured Village," 39
Conservation Area,
    Ball's Falls, 182
    Cave Springs, 185
    Comfort Maple, 182
    Jordan Harbour, 182, 184

Louth, 184
Mountainview, 184
Rockway, 184
St. John's, 184
Virgil Dam and Reservoir, 184
Wainfleet Bog, 180
Wainfleet Wetlands, 180–181
Woodend, 185, 197
Conservation Authorities Act of 1946, 180
Cornwall, Levi, 159
Coughtry, Graham, 105
Cranmer, Doug, 33
Criminal Code, 1982, 91
Crysler, Harmanus, 55, 88
Curnoe, Greg, 105

Darling and Pearson, Architects, 81–82
Darling, John, 165
Davis, Saul, 88
Decaire, Daniel, 22
DeCew House, 32, 135, 197
Decou, John, 135
de la Rue, Warren, 22
Dodson, Laura, 157
Dolson, Isaac, 63, 65
Dominion Public Building, 227
Doran–Marshall Residence, 157
Doran, W.L., 158
Drew, John, 157
Drummond Hill Cemetery, 134, 174
Drummondville, 147–148
Dufferin Islands, 191

Edison, Thomas, 22
English, Jay, 102
Erie Canal, 70, 215

Erie Peat Company, 232
Evans, Matthew, 22

Fallsview Casino, 54, 92, 95
Federation of Ontario Naturalists, 195
Fenian Brotherhood, 135, 138
First Nations Peace Monument, 32
FitzGibbon, Lieutenant James, 128, 135, 197
Floral Clock, 144–145
Formal Gardens, 187–192
Forsyth, William, 55, 87
Fort
    Drummond, 133
    Erie, 135, 173
    George, 126, 131, 133–134, 172
    Mississauga, 133
Freedom Park, 36
French, Kristen, 192
Fry House, 80
Fry, Jacob, 80
Fugitive Slave Act, 37
Fuller, Thomas, 227

Glasgow-Fortner House, 161
Glen Elgin, 163–165, 167
Glencairn Hall, 155–156
Glenview Mansion, 157, 172
Grandview Manor, 160
Great Gorge Route, 227
Great Wolf Lodge, 96–97
Gretzky, Wayne, 113–114
Grimsby Park, 171

Hamilton, Alexander, 156
Hamilton, John, 155–156
Hamilton, Robert, 63, 69, 147
Harry, Gord, 204

Haunted Niagara, 172–174
Head, Sir Francis Bond, 38
Hennepin, Louis, 11
Hill, Red, 52
Hobson, Joseph, 228
Homer, Village of, 165–166
Hornblower, 28, 48, 51
Hotels, 55–61
    Appletree Inn, 60
    Clifton House, 56, 88
    Crown Plaza Hotel *see* General Brock
    Europa, 81
    General Brock, 57
    Henry of Pelham Inn, 118
    Hilton Fallsview, 56
    Moffat Inn, 60
    Oban Inn, 60
    Old Bank House, 59
    Olde Angel Inn, 58–59, 66–67, 172
    Old Stone Inn, 56–57
    Pillar and Post, 59–60
    Prince of Wales, 60–61, 66–67, 173
    Rodman Hall Inn, 154
    South Landing Inn, 69
    Sterling Inn, 58
Hydro-Electric Power Commission of Ontario, 135

Iafrate, Sandra, 107
Imperial Bank of Canada, 73
Incline Railway, Niagara Falls, 48, 51
Indian Council House, 32
Indian Village, Niagara Falls, 29–30
Indigenous Gardens, 32–33

Indigenous Legacy, 27–33
Indigenous Peoples
    Algonquin, 27–28
    Haundenosaunee, 28, 31
    Hurons, 28
    Iroquois, 27–28
Indigenous Warriors Monument, 135–136
International Nickel Company of Canada, 73
International Silver Factory, 82

Jockey Club, Fort Erie, 95
John Thompson House, 148
Jones, Augustus, 142
Jones, James, 59
Jones, Morgan and Julie, 60
Jordan Harbour, 167
Jordan Station, 80, 203–204, 228
Jordan Village, 79–80, 107
Jouppien, Jon, 161

Keefer Mansion *see* Maplehurst
King, William Lyon Mackenzie, 212
Kurelek, William, 104

Lake House, 160
Lakeside Pottery, 107
Landscape of Nations Memorial, 26, 31, 131–132, 144
Larkin, John D., 156
Latshaw, John, 155
Laura Secord Homestead, 144
Lennox, E.J., 22
Lighthouse Festival, 104, 160
Little Africa, 37
Living Water Wayside Chapel, 143
Locomoland, 90

Locust Grove Picnic Area, 18, 145
Longs Hotel *see* Hotel, Prince of Wales
Looff, Charles, 192
Loring, Frances, 149, 212
Lower Steel Arch Bridge *see* Bridges, Whirlpool Rapids
Lost Villages and Ghost Towns, 163–175
Lotus Grove, 144
Lundy's Lane, 129, 136–137, 141, 147–148, 151
Lundy's Lane Historical Society, 29

MacGregor, John, 105
Mackenzie, William Lyon, 69, 146, 165
Magic Winery Bus, 118–119
Madison, James, 127
Maguire, Molly, 173
Maid of the Mist, 28, 48
Main Streets, Historic, 63–83
Mansion House, 77
Maplehurst, 158, 161
Maple Leaf Place, 44
Martin, William, 78
Mary Morton Tours, 119
Mather, Robert, 212
Mather, Alonzo Clark, 147, 150, 212
McFarland House, 17, 135, 159
Merritt, Thomas Rodman, 153–154, 192
Merritt, William Hamilton, 153–154, 192, 215
Merritton Tunnel, 170, 174
Mewinhza Archaeology Gallery, 32
Milloy, Duncan, 60

Moffat, Richard, 60
Monroe, Marilyn, 47, 57, 102, 212
Moody, Alan, 92
Morningstar Mill, 197, 199
Morningstar, Wilson, 197
Moseby, Solomon, 38
Museum,
    Battle Ground Hotel, 136
    Fort Erie Railway, 232
    Gale Family War of 1812 Gallery, 136
    Morningstar Mill, 197
    Niagara Falls History, 136
    Niagara Railway, 232
    Niagara Military, 136
    RiverBrink, 105
    St. Catharines, 77, 221
    Willoughby Historical, 146

NAACP, 38, 168
Navy Island, 32, 146
Neutral Confederacy, 28
Newark *see* Niagara-on-the-Lake
Niagara (movie), 47, 57, 102, 212
Niagara Airbus, 118
Niagara Baptist Church Burial Ground, 38
Niagara Circles, 169–171
Niagara College, 33, 111
Niagara Day Tours, 118
Niagara Electric Power Company, 22
Niagara Escarpment, 15–17
Niagara Falls
    City of, 80–82
    Evolution of, 15–25
    International Camp Meeting Association, 172
    Park Act, 44

Niagara Glen, 18–20, 144
Niagara Glen Reserve, 200
Niagara Movement *see* NAACP
Niagara-on-the-Lake, 38, 59–60, 63–67, 102–103, 107, 135, 171, 224–225
Niagara-on-the-Lake wineries, 120–121
Niagara Parks,
    Botanical Garden, 187–188
    Butterfly Conservatory, 188–189
    Commission, 22, 32–33, 51, 89, 142, 187–188, 190–191, 227
    Floral Display House, 51
    Power Station, 23, 25, 51, 174
    School of Horticulture, 144, 188
Niagara Parkway, 142–147
Niagara Peninsula Conservation Authority, 180
Northern Dancer (horse), 96
Norton Cabin, 30, 60
Norton, Annette, 174
Norton, John, 30, 32, 128, 130, 132, 136, 160
Norton's Grove, 32

Oak Hall, 154–155
Oak Hill, 154
Oakes, Eunice, 154
Oakes, Harry, 154–155
Old Lock One Commons, 71–72
Old Scow Lookout Point, 44, 51–52
Olmstead, Frederick Law, 191–192
Oneida Tower, 92
Ontario Grape Growing and Wine Manufacturing Company, 111
Ontario Hydro, 24

Ontario Peat Company, 180
Ontario Power Generation, 24, 51
Ossuary, 28–30
Outlets, Shopping, 83

Paradise Grove Oak Savannah Restoration Area, 187–188
Park,
    Crystal Beach Amusement, 169–170
    Erie Beach Amusement, 167–168
    Jaycee Gardens, 192
    Lakeside, 192
    Montebello, 191–192
    Queenston Heights, 18, 130, 132, 196
    Queen Victoria, 47–49, 51, 89, 141, 188, 190
    Short Hills Provincial, 204
Pelee Island, 110
Perry, Matthew, 57
Peterson, Tanya Jean, 107
Point Abino Lighthouse, 219–220
Port Colborne, 72–74, 104, 159–160, 219–220, 221, 230
    Club, 159
    Harbour Railway *see* Railways, Trillium
Port Dalhousie, 70–72, 217
Port Dover, 104
Port Robinson, 78–79, 219–220
Portage Road, 147–148
Powell, John, 173
Power Plant,
    Queenston-Chippawa Hydro-electric, 23
    Robert Moses, 24
    Sir Adam Beck, 23–24

    Toronto Generating Station Electric, 22
Power Station, William Birch Rankine, 174
Prospect House, 55, 88
Puss n Boots (horse), 96

Quebec Bank, 69, 78
Queen Elizabeth Way (QEW), 149–151
Queen Victoria Place Restaurant, 49, 51, 187
Queenston, 67–69, 105, 135

Race Track, Fort Erie, 95–96
Raid on Short Hills, 165
Railroad *see* Railway and Railroad
Railway and Railroad
    Buffalo, Brantford and Goderich Railway, 229–230
    Canada Southern Railway, 89, 224, 228
    Canadian National Railway, 230–231
    Erie and Niagara Railway 89, 156, 224
    Erie and Ontario Railway, 223
    Erie Peat Railway, 231
    Grand Trunk Railway, 81, 170, 174, 203–204, 229
    Great Gorge Railway, 227
    Great Western Railway, 11, 80–82, 89, 164, 167, 174, 203, 228
    Michigan Central Railroad, 171, 226
    New York Central Railroad, 229

Niagara Falls Park and River Railway, 188, 198, 227
Niagara, St. Catharines and Toronto Railway, 192
Port Colborne Harbour Railway, 231
Snake Hill and Pacific Railway, 167
Toronto, Hamilton and Buffalo Railway, 228–229
Trillium Railway, 231
Welland Railway, 231
Rainbow Tower, 47
Ramblers Rest Pavilion, 48
Rankine, William Birch, 22
Richardson, Arthur Herbert, 179–180
Richardson, Samuel, 154, 192
Ridgeway, 80
Robin Hood Flour, 73, 220
Rodman Hall, 152–153, 192
Roebling, John, 211
Romance, Trisha, 107
Rorback, Andrew, 148
Rorback's Tavern *see* Whirlpool House
Roselawn, 159–160
Royal Visits,
    King George VI (1939), 48, 148, 211
    Marquess of Lorne (1879), 51
    Prince Alexander of Yugoslavia (2005), 59
    Princess Katherine of Yugoslavia (2005), 59
    Prince George VI (1927), 212
    Prince of Wales (1860), 49, 67, 136

Prince of Wales, Edward VIII (1902, 1927), 59, 60, 212
Princess of Wales (1902), 59
Princess Louise (1879), 49
Queen Elizabeth, Queen Mother, (1939), 148, 211
Queen Elizabeth II (1973), 60, 102–103
Roy Terrace, 18

Salem Chapel *see* Bethel Chapel
Schiller, Johann, 110
School of Restoration Arts, 69, 157
Screaming Tunnel, 174, 197
Secord, David, 116
Secord, James, 117
Secord, Laura, 32, 116–117, 124–125, 128, 135–136, 197
Servos, Jacob, 32
Seward, William and Susannah, 39
Shaw Festival, 67, 101–104
Sheaffe, General Sir Roger Hale, 13, 136
Sherwood, Teri, 33
Silvertown, 82–83
Simcoe, John Graves, 35, 63
Six Nations of the Grand River First Nation, 30–31
Skye-Grandmond, Leona, 33
Skylon Tower, 92
Slater, Robert Peter, 157
Smith, Nicholas, 117
Smith, W.H., 147
Snow, Michael, 105
Solid Comfort, Port Colborne, 74, 230
Somerville, William Lyon, 149

South Landing Inn, 69
Statue,
    Brant, John, 31, 132
    Brock, Isaac, 130
    George VI, King, 49
    Norton, John, 31, 131
    Shaw, George Bernard, 100
    Tesla, Nikola, 51, 53
St. Catharines, 75–76, 191–192
St. David's, 117
St. David's Buried Gorge, 20, 145
Steelton, 79
St. John's West, 165–166
Steward, William, 38
Steward Home, 38
Stone, Colonel Isaac, 139
St. Urban Estates *see* Wineries, Vineyard Estates
Swan, Joseph, 22

Table Rock, 20, 51, 57
Table Rock Centre, 44–45, 55
Table Rock House, 44, 51, 88, 227
Table Rock Museum 87, 44
Taylor, E.P., 95–96
Tecumseh, 128
Temporale, Louis, 49
Ten Thousand Buddhas Sarira Stupa Temple, 44–45
Tesla, Nikola, 22, 51
Teslatron, 94
Theatre,
    Avalon, 95, 102
    Court House, 67
    Festival, 102–103
    Lighthouse Festival, 104, 159
    Oakes Garden, 47, 190–191
    Roselawn, 104
    Royal George, 102–104

Seneca Queen, 102
Showboat Festival, 104, 160
Thom, Ronald, 103
Thomas, William, 130
Thomson, John Jr., 148
Thompson, William A., 156
Thorold, 77-78, 135, 216-217
Toronto Power Generating Station, 23
Totem, St. Catharines', 33
Trail,
    Bert Lowe Side, 198
    Bruce, 195-199
    DeCew Loop, 200
    Friendship, 230
    General Brock Side, 198
    Gord Harry, 204, 231
    Laura Secord Legacy, 197, 198-199
    Niagara Glen, 19, 200, 202, 205
    Merritt Trail, 202
    Twenty Valley, 202-204
    Upper Canada Heritage, 226
    Welland Canal Parkway, 220-221
Treaty of Ghent, 130
Tubman, Harriet, 37-38, 77
Tully, Kivas, 75
Turtle Island, 27

Underground Railroad, 35-38, 154, 160
Upside Down House, 90

Urquhart, Tony, 105
Vintners Quality Alliance (VQA), 111
Vin Villa, 110-111
Voices of Freedom Park, 35, 38-39

Walker Botanical Garden and Arboretum, 188, 192
Wallenda, Nik, 47-48
War of 1812, 32, 115, 127-130, 133, 142, 147, 175
Waters, Daniel, 39
WEGO buses, 233
Weir, Samuel E., 105
Welland, 74-75, 105, 218
    Art Gallery of, 105
    Canal, 70-71, 215-221, 223
    County Court House, 75-76
    Mills, 78
    Murals, 74-75
Wesley, George, 39
Wesley, Winnifred, 39
Wesley Park, 172
Westinghouse, George, 22
Whirlpool Aero Car, 17
Whirlpool House, 148
White Water Walk, 20, 45, 201-202
WildPlay Niagara, 145
Willowbank, 69, 156-158
Wilmott, Charles M., 67
Wilson, Charles, 55

Wilson's Tavern *see* Prospect House
Wine Country, 109-123
Wineries, 109-123
Wineries, individual
    Cave Spring Vineyard, 80, 111, 107, 120, 122, 185
    Château des Charmes, 111-112
    Wayne Gretzky Estates, 113, 120
    Henry of Pelham Family Estate Winery, 117-118, 122
    Inniskillin Niagara Estate Winery, 111, 117-118, 120, 143
    Palatine Hills Estate Winery, 113, 115, 120
    Peller Estates Winery, 113, 115
    Ravine Vineyard Estate Winery, 116, 120
    Reif Estate Winery, 115, 120
    Vineyard Estates, 111
Wineries, list of in
    Niagara-on-the-Lake, 120-121
    Niagara region, 122-123
Wine Tours, 118-119
Wismer, Elizabeth, 80
Wood, Wyn, 49
Woodward, Henry, 22
Wyle, Florence, 212

Zeidler, Eberhard, 95
Zimmermann, Ron and Barb, 107

PHOTO CREDITS

All photos © Ron Brown, except as listed below.

ALAMY STOCK PHOTO

eugen: 150.
Performance Image: 26–27, 29.
Pictorial Press Ltd: 47 (left).
Rubens Abboud: 88.

SHUTTERSTOCK

alwayssunnyalwaysreal: 114–115.
A. Michael Brown: 220.
AnjelikaGr: 49.
arindambanerjee: 47 (right).
CEW: 208–209.
EB Adventure Photography: 210.
elargetoianu: 206–207.
Elena Berd: 116–117.
Elena Elisseeva: 110 (top).
eskystudio: 108–109, 113, 119 (top).
Fabian Junge: 130.
Gilberto Mesquita: 91, 106.
Haitao Ran: 176–177.
HansTischlerFoto: 19.
James Kirkikis: 36.
Janice Chen: 41–42.
Javen: 46.
JHVEPhoto: 83, 97, 112 (bottom), 114 (bottom), 117 (bottom), 143, 159, 186–187.
Joanne Dale: 34–35, 58–59, 137, 152–153.
Joel S. Fetzer: 146.
Jon Nicholls Photography: 98–99, 110 (bottom), 151, 216.
jrtwynam: 170, 175, 183.
Kiev.Victor: 126–127.
KissCat: 8.
Kit Leong: 50.
ksana05: 221.
lastdjedai: 84–85.
Leah Husbands: 200–201.
Lenush: 111 (top).
Locomotive74: 222–223.
Manu M Nair: 189.
Marc Kirouac: 213.
MatthewDWilliams: 168–169.
mshirani: 178–179.
NiagaraSnap: 205.
Paul McKinnon: 86–87.
Pim van der Maden: 66.
Rabsanity: 203.
Reimar: 124–125.
Russ Heinl: 214–215.
Sharlyn: 145.
Shawn.ccf: 48, 89.
Simply Photos: 185.
Sketchart: 14–15, 173.
S.M.Lens: 135.
sockagphoto: 61, 102–103.
Songquan Deng: 140–141.
Spiroview Inc: 100–101.
Tom Worsley: 194–195.
Vadim 777: 6–7.
Vadim Rodnev: 65.
Vintagepix: 119 (bottom).
Wangkun Jia: 92–93.
Wirestock Creators: 162–163.